TASTE TESTED AND APPROVED 3

Transforming Healthy Home Cooked Meals into Gluten Free Goodness the Whole Family Will Love; Whether They Eat Gluten Free or Not!

TASTE-TEMPTING BREADS, BREAKFAST, DESSERTS, AND SWEETS

Janeen Pond

TASTE TESTED AND APPROVED 3 -- Transforming Healthy Home Cooked Meals into Gluten Free Goodness the Whole Family Will Love; Whether They Eat Gluten Free or Not! --TASTE-TEMPTING BREADS, BREAKFAST, DESSERTS, AND SWEETS

Copyright © 2015 Janeen Pond, Tooele, Utah

ISBN-13: 978-1512115819
ISBN-10: 1512115819

TESTIMONIALS

"I have been a neighbor and friend of Janeen Pond for 10 years and have had many delicious breads, cakes, cookies, and desserts for both regular eaters and gluten free eaters. Everything Janeen makes is made from scratch with love and a passion for healthy food and her desire to share and help others." ...Julie Chapman

Janeen has a talent for making recipes go from ordinary to extraordinary. My family loves trying new recipes and this book has plenty to offer. We have not been disappointed! ...Janelle Ayala

"Janeen has great ideas and is a great cook. These recipes will make your meals memorable." ...Judi Sorensen

DEDICATIONS

To my husband, my children, their spouses, and my grandchildren

who make my life such a joy to live and to always cook for.

You've encouraged me and helped me learn that I can "Do Hard Things".

Dreams can become reality!

THANK YOU!

Putting together this book is not an individual endeavor. Yes, I have done tons by myself, but I have had to have the support of my husband, Nick, to allow me the hours to do this. He was also my "guinea pig" and had to taste all the recipes and help me rate them. I am so grateful for my mother, grandmother, daughters, friends, teachers, and all who have inspired along the way and taught me how to cook and encouraged me along the way.

I am also thankful for SherLynne Beach who has helped put this whole book together. She has the knowledge that I never will. She makes it all look professional. Thank you all again for helping me accomplish this goal that I have had. My dream has now become a reality!

My children are my prize treasures in life as well as my grandchildren. They have encouraged me to keep going with this project and helped me fix things on the computer. I have cooked many dinners for them and I've always wanted to make them happy when they came to Grandma's. Thank you for being there for me and supporting me! Love you forever!

TABLE OF CONTENTS

INTRODUCTION

It has taken my whole life thus far, to accomplish enough skills in cooking to be able to want to share my recipes with you. I am not a gourmet cook by any means, but I have always loved to cook. Cooking wonderful tasting food that has great flavor is very enjoyable to me. I love to mix-it-up and cook all kinds of food with different flavors. Trying a new recipe almost daily is very common for me. After preparing them, each receives a satisfaction rating which helps me determine if I ever want to cook that recipe again. Hence the name, Taste Tested and Approved!

When I was first married, I cooked simple down-home cooking like I saw my mother cook. Not a week went by that I wasn't calling her and asking her for recipes and how to cook this and how to do that. I have included some of these favorites from the early years that I cooked for my young family---fast and easy to put on the table with 5 busy children. They maybe wouldn't meet the culinary requirements of today's standards, but I have changed with the times and cook differently than I did in the 70's.

I have always loved cooking ever since I was little. I loved good tasting food! My Grandma Smith was a good cook. I loved her Raisin-filled Sugar Cookies that were always in the cookie jar when I visited! She made the best dinner rolls, cinnamon rolls, pies, and much more too. I used to say to myself that I wanted to be just like my mother and grandmother and be a good cook. I had a goal and I have been working on it ever since.

My mother learned from her mother and then I in turn, learned from my mother! I took Home Economics classes in school and then majored in Home Economics in College. My dream and goal was to teach others to cook and show them how. I have had many opportunities to do this in my life. I am still doing this as I teach herb and vegetable classes to the community for the Master Gardeners Association in my state.

These recipes are my collection of the dishes that earned a great rating when I prepared them for my family. Everyone has different tastes and they like some things and not others. I hope you will find some food inspiration from this book that you will want to add to your collection to serve your family.

Have fun cooking and, of course, tasting! Enjoy!

HOW TO USE THIS BOOK

When I started to cook, I was not allergic to anything that I knew of----but life happens and I am now celiac and can't eat wheat, barley or rye and only gluten free oats. It so happens that my husband, some of my children, grandchildren, and close relatives also have the same problem, so it is easy for me to cook for us. I now cook gluten free and so lots of my recipes and the ones I am drawn towards are ones that I can eat or are easy to alter to gluten free.

I have included many desserts, cookies, pies, etc. that were not gluten free, but were my favorites for years and years. They can be converted to gluten free, however, if you have to eat that way. In the Gluten Free Substitutions Section I have included a conversion chart that lets you see just how to do this----so you can convert any recipe ...almost! I have not changed all of them to gluten free, but you can if you need too. Some recipes cannot be changed since they use whole wheat flour or are rolled doughs that can't be rolled very well with gluten free dough etc.

I wanted to have those who don't have eating allergies to also be able to use this book also. I have listed the normal ingredients in the recipes, and in parentheses I have used the letters (GF) for ingredients to watch out for. The letters "GF" mean that you need to use Gluten Free ingredients. Just make sure that you read the labels and only use Gluten Free products. An example is soy sauce. Most brands have wheat in them, but some don't. Use the brands that don't.

In conclusion, I have attempted to make a recipe book that all can use. If you have other allergies, such as dairy, nuts, or soy etc., I hope that you will know how to change the recipes since you are living that way daily. Use other kinds of milk, no nuts, other flours, and don't use soy sauce but coconut aminos can be used instead for soy sauce. Use the egg replacements, if needed, for you, too. I am only allergic to wheat, barley, rye and some nuts so I just steer clear of them and I am good to go.

Happy Converting!

BREAKFAST ANYONE?

CEREAL

GRANDMA GUNDRY'S GRANOLA

8 cups rolled old-fashioned oats (GF)

6 cups rolled wheat (can substitute GF oats)

2 cups wheat germ, untoasted (use GF oat bran or flax seed meal)

1-1/2 to 2 cups of flaked coconut

2 tsp. salt

1-1/2 to 2 cups brown sugar

1 cup oil

1 cup water

2-3 tsp. vanilla

Options: nuts, raisins etc.

1. Mix salt, brown sugar oil, water, and vanilla together. Pour over the mixed dry ingredients.

2. Bake in a turkey roaster type pan at 225 degrees; until crisp but not too brown. Stir this every 30 minutes to distribute. It usually takes about 2 hours or more to get crisp.

3. Add raisins and nuts after cooking, if using. Store this in refrigerator for a longer shelf life.

INSTANT OATMEAL MIX

2 cups quick oatmeal (GF)

1/2 cup firmly packed brown sugar

1/2 tsp. cinnamon

1/2 cup instant dry milk

You may add dried fruit---dates, apples, bananas, nuts, raisins, etc.

1. Combine all ingredients in a heavy duty ziploc bag.   Yield: 3 cups oatmeal mix

2. To serve: Pour boiling water over desired amount of oatmeal, barely covering mixture.   Stir and let stand 2 minutes. Adjust water amount and cereal to desired consistency.

3. To Microwave: Boil 3/4 cup water 1 to 2 minutes, then stir in 2/3 cup oatmeal mix, and cook 30 seconds. Let stand 1 minute. Enjoy!

BO BO'S GLUTEN FREE SCRUMDIDLYUMPTIOUS GRANOLA

8 cups gluten free rolled oats

6 cups of your favorite GF cereal (GF Chex cereals, corn flakes, Mesa Sunrise)

2 cups flax seed meal

2 cups coconut

2 cups packed brown sugar

1 - 2 Tbs. cinnamon

1 cups nuts - sunflower seeds, unsalted or raw slivered almonds, or pecans

1 cup craisins, banana chips, dried apples, raisins, or a mixture

1 cup oil

1 cup water

2 tsp. salt

1 Tbs. vanilla (or use maple flavoring for a Maple-pecan & craisin granola)

1. Mix oats, cereal, flax seed, coconut, brown sugar, and cinnamon in a large bowl.

2. Mix oil, water, salt, and vanilla in a separate bowl. Pour wet ingredients over dry ingredients and mix well.

3. Spread evenly in a large roaster pan or onto 2 large sided baking pans.

4. Bake at 225 degrees for 2 - 5 hours. Stir every 30 minutes until crisp but not too brown.

5. Mix in nuts and dried fruit at the end of cooking. Enjoy!

WHOLE WHEAT CEREAL

If you don't have access to a grinder to crack wheat for cereal, just cook the wheat kernels whole.

1 cup whole wheat kernels

3 cups water

Salt for the water

1. Boil 1 cup of whole wheat kernels in salted water for about 30 to 45 minutes. Vary the cooking time depending on how soft you want the kernels. They should be chewy and not tough.

2. Drain and store covered in your refrigerator for up to a week.

3. To use, heat a bowl of kernels in your microwave oven. Add raisins, nuts, oatmeal, fruit, etc. for variety. Enjoy!

TRAVIS'S GRANOLA – REGULAR OR GLUTEN FREE

8 cups rolled oats (GF)

1-1/2 cups wheat germ or flax seed meal (GF)

1-1/2 cups oat bran or rice bran (GF)

2 cups flaked coconut

1 cup sunflower seeds

1 cup finely chopped almonds

1 cup finely chopped pecans

1 cup finely chopped walnuts

1-1/2 tsp. salt

1/2 cup brown sugar

1/4 cup maple syrup

3/4 cup honey

1 cup oil or use 1/2 c. applesauce & 1/2 cup oil

1 tsp. cinnamon

1 tsp. vanilla

2 cups raisins or dried cranberries

1. Preheat oven to 325 degrees. Line 2 large sided baking sheets with parchment or foil.

2. Combine oats, wheat germ, oat bran, sunflower seeds, almonds, pecan, and walnuts in a large bowl.

3. Stir together the salt, brown sugar, maple syrup, honey, oil, cinnamon and vanilla in a saucepan. Bring to a boil over medium heat, then pour over the dry ingredients and stir to coat. Spread mixture own evenly on baking sheets.

4. Bake in the oven until crispy; about 20 minutes or more. Stir halfway through. Cool; then stir in raisins or dried cranberries before storing in an airtight container.

SLOW COOKER OATMEAL

1 cup milk, plus more for serving

1-2 Tbs. brown sugar, plus more for serving

1/2 tsp. vanilla

1/2 tsp. cinnamon

1/4 tsp. salt

1 Tbs. ground flax seed meal (optional)

4 cups water

1 cup steel-cut oats (use GF oats)

2 apples, peeled, cored and cut into 1-inch pieces

2 Tbs. butter, cut into small pieces

Additional toppings such as: raisins, nuts, crasins, milk, more sugar, etc., if desired.

1. Generously grease with shortening the inside of a 5 to 6 quart slow cooker

2. Add milk, sugar, vanilla, cinnamon, flax, salt and 4 cups water to slow cooker. Add oats; stir, and add apples. Mix together.

3. Cook, covered on low for 8 hours until oats and apples are tender. Some oats will stick to sides. Stir the oats and serve 6 hungry people.

4. Add additional toppings such as: raisins, nuts, crasins, milk, more sugar, etc., if desired.

CRACKED WHEAT CEREAL

1/2 tsp. salt

3 cups water

1 cup Cracked Wheat

1. In a 2 qt. saucepan bring water and salt to a boil; add cracked wheat, stir, & turn heat down.

2. Simmer covered for about 15-20 minutes, stirring occasionally.

3. Serve with milk and honey. Add fruit or nuts to your cereal to increase nutrition and jump start your morning, if desired. Yield: 4 servings

CROCK POT OATMEAL - Steel-Cut Oat recipe is in parenthesis

2 cups old fashioned oats – (or use 1-1/2 cups steel-cut oats) - (use GF)

6 cups water – (or use 4 cups water and 2 cups milk)

Dash of salt (optional) – (or 1/4 tsp. salt)

1 teaspoon cinnamon (optional)

handful dried fruit of choice (optional)

1. Put everything into a greased large capacity slow cooker and stir well.

2. Turn on Low and go to bed for 7 to 8 hours. (With steel-cut oats cook 4 hours on low and 4 hours on warm.) In the morning, give it a stir before serving.

3. Older kids and adults can serve themselves adding toppings of their choice from milk, to fresh fruit and honey. It's up to your individual tastes.

BREAKFAST CASSEROLES, FRITTATAS, EGGS...

CHRISTMAS MORNING BREAKFAST –

We've had this every year since my children were little

6 slices bread, buttered on both sides (use GF)

2 cups diced ham, cooked sausage or bacon - sausage is our favorite

6 eggs, beaten

2 cups milk

2 cups shredded cheddar cheese

Salt and pepper

1. Place buttered bread in 9 x 13 casserole pan and then sprinkle on meat of your choice.

2. Beat eggs, add milk, and season with salt and pepper.

3. Pour over meat and then sprinkle on cheese. Cover with foil and refrigerate overnight.

4. Bake the next morning at 350 degrees for 50 minutes; until cooked through in the middle.

5. Enjoy!

HASHBROWN BREAKFAST CASSEROLE

Crust:

6 cups shredded hash brown potatoes; thawed

1 tsp. salt

1/2 tsp. pepper

1 stick butter, melted

Filling:

2 cups mild cheddar, shredded

6 eggs, beaten

2 cups half and half

1-1/2 cups meat or veggies or any combo of them -*ideas are listed below*

6 green onions; minced

1/2 tsp. pepper or hot sauce

Salt to taste

1. Preheat oven to 450 degrees. In a large bowl, combine all crust ingredients to make the crust. Turn into a 9 x 13-inch greased pan. Use your fingers to press it onto the bottom and up the sides to form a crust.

2. Bake about 25 minutes. You want the crust to be very crispy so cook it longer if needed, but watch it so it doesn't burn.

3. Remove from oven and reduce oven temperature to 350 degrees.

4. Meanwhile, mix filling ingredients together and pour over the crust.

5. Bake at 350 degrees for 30 minutes or until lightly golden brown. Great served with fruit and muffins.

NOTE:
- ✓ *This recipe can cut in half and cooked in a pie pan or doubled and cooked in a large sided sheet pan.*
- ✓ *You can also make this a <u>day ahead,</u> but keep the baked crust separate from the filling so it is not soggy. When ready to bake, just pour in the filling and bake 30 minutes*

SUGGESTION:
- ✓ <u>*Combinations to try:*</u> *(a) Swiss cheese, bacon, and green onions; (b) Monterey Jack cheese, broccoli and white onion; (c) Gruyere cheese, roasted red peppers and shallots; (d) Feta cheese, fresh spinach leaves, and Vidalia onion; (e) ham, green onion, and Monterey Jack cheese; (f) broccoli, sharp cheese, and shallots, or (g) use your own favorite flavors!*

CROCK-POT MORNING CASSEROLE

1 27 to 32-oz. bag frozen hash brown potatoes

1 lb. sausage, bacon, or ham; diced; cooked and drained

1 medium diced onion

1 green or red pepper; diced

2 cups shredded cheddar or Monterey Jack cheese

1 dozen eggs, beaten

1 cup milk

1 tsp. salt

1 tsp. pepper

1. Grease a 5 qt. slow-cooker. Place a layer of frozen potatoes on the bottom.

2. Follow with a layer of bacon, onions, green peppers and cheese. Repeat the layers two or three times, ending with a layer of cheese.

3. Beat eggs, milk, salt, and pepper together. Pour over slow-cooker mixture; cover. Cook on Low 10-12 hours.

GREEN BEAN, HAM, AND CHEESE FRITTATA

Or another vegetable of choice like Asparagus

2 tsp. olive oil

1 pound green beans or asparagus; cut in 1-inch pieces

1/2 pound thinly sliced deli ham, cut in strips

2 bunches (12-16) scallions cut in 1-inch pieces

8 large eggs

1 tsp. salt

1/4 tsp. pepper

1 cup shredded Fontina or Mozzarella cheese

1. Preheat oven to 350 degrees. Heat the oil in a 10-inch non-stick ovenproof skillet over medium heat. Add green beans, ham, and scallions.

2. Cover and cook until beans are crisp-tender, about 6 minutes.

3. In a large bowl, whisk eggs, 1 tsp. salt and 1/4 tsp. pepper; add the cheese. Add to skillet and tilt to distribute evenly. Gently press down on vegetables to cover them with eggs.

4. Cook without stirring until edges are slightly set; about 1 minute.

5. Bake in oven until center is set about 25 to 30 minutes. Run a spatula or wooden spoon around edges, slide frittata onto a plate. Cut into 4 wedges.

SPINACH AND BACON FRITTATA

6 large eggs

1 cup ricotta or cottage cheese

1/4 cup parmesan cheese

Salt and Pepper

5 strips bacon, cut into 1/2–inch pieces

5 boiled potatoes, quartered

2 bunches spinach (about 10 ounces each), washed, trimmed, and roughly chopped

1 cup shredded cheddar cheese – optional

1. Preheat oven to 350 degrees. In a medium bowl, whisk eggs, ricotta, parmesan, 1 tsp. salt and 1/4 tsp. pepper.

2. In a medium nonstick ovenproof skillet, cook bacon until crisp, 6-7 minutes. Drain all but 1 tsp. of fat from pan. Add potatoes and cook until warmed through, 2-3 minutes.

3. Add spinach and toss until barely wilted.

4. Add egg mixture and stir until slightly thickened, about 1 minute.

5. Bake in oven until center is set, about 15 minutes. (I have also put 1 cup cheddar cheese on top when I take it out of the oven and let it melt.) Cut into 4 wedges. Enjoy!

OVEN-BAKED SPANISH TORTILLA

2 Tbs. olive oil, plus more the baking dish

1 lb. Yukon gold potatoes; cut into 1/2–inch pieces

4 scallions—chop the white parts and slice the dark green part

1 medium red pepper; cut into 1/4-inch pieces

1 tsp. crushed red pepper—optional

Salt and pepper

10 large eggs

1 cup sour cream

6 oz. extra sharp cheddar cheese, grated (1-1/2 cups)

1/2 cup grated Parmesan (2 oz.)

1. Heat oven to 375 degrees. Lightly oil a 2 quart baking dish.

2. Place the potatoes in a saucepan and cover with cold water and add 1/2 tsp. salt. Bring to a boil and cook until potatoes are tender, 5-7 minutes. Drain and set aside.

3. Meanwhile, chop the scallions and separate the white and green parts. Heat the 2 Tbs. of oil in a skillet.

4. Add the chopped white parts of the scallions, red pepper, garlic and crushed red pepper; cook until tender, 5 to 6 minutes. Add potatoes and combine. Transfer all to the baking dish.

5. In a large bowl, whisk the eggs and sour cream. Stir in the cheeses, sliced dark green parts of the scallions and 1/2 tsp. each of salt and pepper. Stir to mix. Bake until puffed and golden brown and just set in the center, 35 to 40 minutes. Let rest for 10 minutes before serving.

POTATO FRITTATA

1 lb. Yukon gold or russet potatoes, scrubbed and thinly sliced 1/8-inch thick

2 Tbs. olive oil

2 large carrots, sliced 1/8 inch thick

Additional optional vegetables: **chopped red pepper, mushrooms, asparagus, etc.**

12 large eggs

1/2 cup sliced green onions

1 small onion, chopped

1/4 tsp. each of salt and pepper

1/2 cup halved cherry tomatoes

1 clove minced garlic

1 Tbs. chopped parsley

1 cup shredded cheddar cheese - optional

1. Preheat oven to 375 degrees. In a 10-inch oven-safe skillet, cook potatoes and chopped onion in hot oil over medium heat for 5 minutes.

2. Add carrots and cook 5 more minutes until browned lightly (At this point I have added chopped red bell pepper, asparagus, mushrooms or what I have on hand to this, if desired.)

3. Mix eggs, salt, pepper and 1/4 cup green onions. Pour over potatoes.

4. Bake in oven 18 minutes; remove and cool for 5 minutes before removing from pan. This is done by inverting it onto a platter. (I have also put 1 cup shredded cheese on top after I have inverted it. Place a pan over it to melt the cheese before adding the tomato mixture.)

5. Mix the other 1/4 cup green onions, tomatoes, garlic and chopped parsley to top; serve.

MINI FRITTATAS

These can be Herb Frittatas by adding 2-3 Tbs. of chopped herbs (parsley, thyme, rosemary or chives)

3 tablespoons melted coconut oil or oil

1 tomato, finely chopped

1 red bell pepper, finely chopped

1 small onion, finely chopped

1 carrot, shredded

8 large eggs, beaten

1/4 teaspoon salt

1. Mix all ingredients together well divide evenly into a large size muffin tin (holds six) which has been coated evenly with melted oil. A tip to coat is to use a paper towel dipped in the melted coconut oil.

2. Bake in a 350 degree oven for about 15 minutes until eggs are thoroughly set. Serve.

VARIATIONS:
- ✓ *Add 2 ounces of any type of cheese.*
- ✓ *Try Feta cheese and chopped spinach for an excellent variation.*
- ✓ *You can also cook these the night before and can be eaten cold the next day.*
- ✓ *One can also mix the mixture the night before, pour into the muffin tins in the morning, and bake for a hot breakfast.*
- ✓ *They can also be wrapped inside some flat bread or a tortilla and taken to eat on the go.*

TUSCAN KALE, OLIVE, AND CARAMELIZED ONION FRITTATA

1 large onion; finely chopped

1 cup sliced mushrooms

2 Tbs. olive oil

12 oz. Tuscan kale (also called Lacinato or dinosaur)

1/4 cup water

8 large eggs

1 cup shredded parmesan cheese, divided

1/2 tsp. salt

1/4 tsp. pepper

12 oil-cured black olives; pitted and slivered or regular black olives

Red chili flakes—optional

1. Preheat broiler with rack 3-4 inches away. In an ovenproof fry pan, cook onion & mushrooms in oil until browned-8-12 min.

2. Add Kale and 1/4 cup water; cook 4-6 min to tender. Whisk eggs, 1/2 cup parmesan cheese, salt, pepper, & olives. Reduce heat to medium, spread out veggies and pour on eggs.

3. Cook until sides are set or about 2 to 3 min (top still looks wet). Sprinkle on 1/2 c. cheese.

4. Broil 3 min. Remove and sprinkle with red chili, if desired.

CRICKET'S BREAKFAST CAKE OR FRITTATA

3-4 Tbs. oil

1 medium onion, diced

1 medium potato, diced

1 zucchini, diced

1 cup broccoli florets

1 tsp. salt, divided

Black pepper

10 eggs

1/2 cup shredded cheddar, Gruyere, or Parmigiano-Reggiano cheese

1. Heat the 3 to 4 Tbs. olive in a large cast-iron pan or non-stick skillet. Add the onion and cook 2 minutes. Add potatoes, zucchini and broccoli; cook; stirring frequently. Cook until the vegetables are tender. Add 1/2 tsp. salt and pepper to taste.

2. Beat the eggs in a bowl. Add remaining 1/2 tsp. salt and pepper to taste. Pour eggs over vegetables and toss. Cook 5 minutes over medium-high heat without stirring.

3. Sprinkle with cheese and cover. Cook until cheese is melted and eggs are completely set. Cut into 8 wedges, just like a cake.

CRUSTLESS TOMATO PIE

1/2 cup milk

1 Tbs. cornstarch

1 (15 oz.) container ricotta or cottage cheese

4 large eggs

1/2 cup chopped basil

1/2 cup grated Parmesan cheese

1/4 cup sliced green onions

1/2 tsp. salt

1 pound sliced tomatoes

1. Whisk 1/2 cup milk and 1 Tbs. cornstarch in large bowl, and then whisk in 1 (15 oz.) container ricotta or cottage cheese, 4 large eggs, 1/2 cup each chopped basil and grated parmesan cheese, 1/4 cup sliced green onions, and 1/2 tsp. salt.

2. Pour into nonstick 10-inch oven-safe skillet and top with 1 lb. sliced tomatoes. Bake at 375 degrees for 35-40 min or until set and puffed. Serves 6

QUICHE LORRAINE

1 8-inch pastry shell, unbaked (use GF) - recipe in pie section of Desserts

3 slices bacon

1 small onion, minced

3/4 cup grated Gruyere or Swiss cheese

1/4 cup grated Parmesan cheese

3 eggs

1 cup light cream

1/2 cup milk

1/2 tsp. salt

Pinch of red pepper

1/8 tsp. nutmeg

1. Cook bacon until crisp; drain. When the bacon is cool, crumble it into bits. Cook the onion in 1 Tbs. bacon fat until transparent. Spread the bacon, onion, and cheese over the pie crust.

2. Beat the eggs slightly; stir in cream, milk, and seasonings. Pour into crust. Bake on a lower shelf in oven at 375 degrees for 40 minutes or until custard does not adhere to the tip of a knife inserted 1 inch from edge. Serves 4

HAM QUICHE

1/2 recipe cream cheese pie pastry (recipe below) - or your favorite one

2 cups Jarlsberg cheese; grated (or use Swiss cheese)

1 heaping cup cubed ham

4 eggs

2 cups half and half

1/2 tsp. dry mustard

1/4 tsp. Worcestershire sauce

Couple dashes hot sauce, such as Tabasco

Parmesan, grated

Pinch freshly grated nutmeg

1. Preheat oven to 400 degrees. Make pie pastry recipe below or your favorite one.

2. Roll pastry into a 9-inch disc and press into pie pan. Cut off loose ends; crimp the edge.

3. Scatter cheese over bottom and top with ham. Whisk eggs, cream, Worcestershire, and hot sauce and pour over ham and cheese.

4. Top with Parmesan cheese and grated nutmeg. Bake 40 minutes. Tent the top with foil if browning too much. Let rest at least 30 minutes before serving.

CREAM CHEESE PASTRY DOUGH

8 Tbs. unsalted butter, room temperature

4 ounces cream cheese, room temperature

1/4 cup heavy cream

1-1/2 cups flour plus 2 Tbs. for rolling out dough (use GF mix)

1/2 tsp. salt

1. Mix butter, cream cheese and cream in food processor, mixer, or by hand.

2. Add flour and salt. Process until dough holds together in a ball. Turn dough out onto a well-floured surface.

3. Divide in 2 pieces and wrap in plastic wrap for at least 30 minutes before rolling out. If dough has been chilled overnight, take out 15 minutes before rolling.

4. Roll out dough and form a 12-inch circle. Place in pie pan. Add your favorite filling and bake. Makes 2 crusts or 1 double-crust pie

ITALIAN BAKED EGGS

1 Tbs. oil

1 small onion, diced

3 garlic cloves, minced

1 can (28-oz) of crushed tomatoes

1/2 cup chopped fresh basil, divided

1/4 tsp. salt

1/8 tsp pepper

4 eggs

4 oz. fresh mozzarella, sliced

1. Heat oven to 400 degrees. In a large oven-safe skillet heat the oil over medium heat. Stir in onions and cook 3-5 minutes until softened. Stir in garlic; cook 1 minute.

2. Add tomatoes, 1/4 cup basil, salt and pepper. Reduce heat to medium; simmer 5 minutes.

3. Remove skillet from heat. Crack eggs into sauce, spacing evenly apart. Top with cheese.

4. Bake at 400 degrees on the top rack; about 8 minutes or until whites are set.

5. Remove from oven and scatter 1/4 cup basil on top. Serve immediately with crusty bread.

BISCUITS AND GRAVY

Travis Pond

1 pound original flavor sausage

1/4 cup butter

1/4 cup flour (use GF) or more

1 quart milk, or more

Salt and lots of pepper, to taste

Hot biscuits -- your favorite recipe

1. Brown in a large skillet; 1 pound original flavor sausage. Remove sausage and retain grease in the pan.

2. To the grease, on medium heat, add 1/4 cup butter to melt and then add 1/4 cup flour (Featherlight GF mix) or more until it's a smooth consistency.

3. Add between 1quart of milk and stir until thickened. Return the meat to pan and season to taste with lots of pepper and salt etc.

4. Serve over hot cooked biscuits, page 89-90.

SPAM AND EGGS BREAKFAST BURRITOS/QUESADILLAS

1 can Spam, cut into 8 slices

Scrambled eggs with cheese for 4 - use about 8 eggs and 1/2 cup cheese

16 corn or flour tortillas

1-1/2 cups or more shredded cheddar cheese

Salsa - optional

1. Panfry the Spam until browned. Drain on a paper towel and set aside.

2. Scramble as many eggs for 4 people that you want (about 8) and add cheese.

3. Meanwhile, cook 2 corn tortillas in another skillet with cheese in the middle (like a quesadilla) until melted. Continue until you have made 8 quesadillas. Keep warm in foil.

4. After cooking, place 1 slice Spam and some eggs in the quesadilla and roll to have your breakfast burrito. Add salsa to it if you wish...I do!   Serves 4 or more

Variation:

✓ *Cube the Spam and panfry. Add the eggs and cheese. Scramble to make scrambled eggs and add cheese. Put on a corn tortilla or just eat the eggs and Spam plain with toast on the side.*

SCRAMBLED EGGS

2 tsp. butter

4 large eggs

Dash of onion powder

Salt & Pepper

1-2 Tbs. water - don't use milk!

1/3 cup shredded cheddar cheese

1. In a skillet over medium heat, melt butter. Add eggs, onion powder, salt & pepper and water.

2. Using a spatula, keep moving the eggs around in the skillet so that they do not overcook and stay moist.

3. Add shredded cheese to taste right before they're done and let it melt. Enjoy!

38

EGG-IN-A-HOLE

Use as many eggs and pieces of bread that you would like

4 slices bread

Butter or oil to spread on bread

1 tsp. oil

4 eggs

Salt and pepper

1. Brush 1 side of each piece of bread with oil or butter. Cut out a hole in the middle of the bread with a round cutter.

2. Heat 1 tsp oil in skillet on medium high heat. Place bread with cut-out oil/butter side up in the pan. Cook 1-2 minutes until crisp. Flip. Crack 1 egg in each hole; season with salt and pepper and cook covered until desired doneness—about 2-3 minutes for runny eggs.

BACON WITH GREASE EGGS

4 slices bacon

4 eggs

1. In a skillet over medium high heat cook 4 slices of bacon, turning <u>often</u> with tongs.

2. When crisp, take out and drain on paper towels. Set aside.

3. Crack 4 eggs into the grease to pan fry until cooked to your liking.

MICROWAVE EGGS IN A CUP

Good for a fast breakfast

2 eggs

2 Tbs. milk

2 Tbs. shredded cheese

Salt and Pepper

1. Spray a 12 oz. microwave safe cup with non-stick spray. Add eggs and milk and beat.

2. Microwave on high 45 seconds; then stir. Microwave another 30-45 seconds until almost set. Top with cheese & salt and pepper. Let cheese melt and eat.

HARD BOILED EGGS

10-12 eggs -- Tip: using eggs near their expiration date are easier to peel after

Water to cover by 1-inch

1. Place raw eggs into a saucepan. Cover by 1-inch with cold water.

2. Cover pan with a lid and bring to a boil. As soon as it boils, turn off the heat and time for 13 minutes.

3. After 13 minutes, uncover, place in the sink and run cold water over them to cool the eggs. Repeat this process of changing the water about 3 times. After they are cool, refrigerate.

SMOOTHIES...

DELICIOUS BREAKFAST SMOOTHIE

1/2 banana

Six frozen strawberries

1/2 cup Greek yogurt

1/2 cup fresh orange juice

1 tablespoon flax seeds

1 egg (optional)

Splash of milk (almond, or real milk, optional)

In a large blender, mix the above ingredients until smooth. Recipe is for one serving. You can double or even quadruple this recipe depending upon how large your blender capacity is. 2.

VARIATIONS:
  ✓ *Change fruit to any fruit you desire.*

GREEN MONSTER SMOOTHIE

Serves 1-2

1 banana, chopped

4 or 5 strawberries

1/2 cup fresh blueberries

1 small peach, peeled & chopped

1 heaping cup fresh spinach

Splash vanilla soy milk

1 Tbsp. Greek yogurt

2 teaspoons honey

1/2 cup crushed ice

1. Place all in blender; blend & serve!

2. (Frozen fruit can also be used, too)

BERRY NUT SMOOTHIE

Serves 1

1 banana

3/4 cup blueberries

3/4 cup milk-dairy or non-dairy

1 Tbsp. nut butter (peanut, almond, etc.)

1. Place all in a blender

2. Blend & serve.

42

DAIRY-FREE BREAKFAST APPLE BERRY SMOOTHIE

Janelle Ayala

1/2 cup So Delicious unsweetened vanilla coconut yogurt

1/3 cup applesauce

3/4 cup pasteurized egg whites

1 pkg. of sugar free or regular apple cider hot drink mix

Dash of vanilla

1-1/2 cup frozen sliced strawberries

1. Blend up

2. Enjoy!

SMOOTHIE

Makes 2 yummy smoothies

2-3 ice cubes

2-3 handfuls of frozen (organic if you can) berries, your choice, about 1 cup total

2 scoops protein powder (I use a vanilla protein powder)

1 cup unsweetened coconut milk (I use So Delicious brand)

1. Place all the ingredients into a blender (I have a 450 watt blender that works great!)

2. Blend. Pour into a glass and enjoy!

PEANUT BUTTER BANANA BREAKFAST SHAKE

Serves 1

1 cup low fat milk

1/2 cup frozen banana slices

1 Tbsp. peanut butter

1/4 tsp. cinnamon

1/2 tsp. vanilla

1. Blend until smooth

2. Serve.

STRAWBERRY BANANA SMOOTHIE

2 cups cold milk

1-1/2 cups frozen strawberries

1 banana

2 Tbs. lemonade concentrate

1. Blend until smooth

2. Serve 2.

IN THE GROOVE GREEN SMOOTHIE

1 banana, peeled and broken into chunks

1 cup seedless green grapes

1/2 Granny Smith apple, peeled, cored and chopped

1 1/2 cups fresh spinach leaves

6 ounces low fat vanilla yogurt

1 scoop protein powder (or serving size suggested on the container)

1. In a blender, process all ingredients until smooth, scraping down the sides of the blender container with a rubber spatula.

2. Pour into 2 glasses and serve.

THE BASIC SMOOTHIE FORMULA!

1/2 cup liquid (milk, water, etc.)

1 cup frozen banana slices

1/2 cup frozen fruit

1/3 cup protein (powders, yogurts, tofu, etc.)

1 cup greens (spinach, kale, etc.)

1 heaping Tbs. of extra health bonuses: (flax seeds, chia seeds, hemp seeds, nut butters, etc.)

1. Blend all together in a blender

2. Blend until smooth, and enjoy!

BERRY SPINACH SMOOTHIE

1 frozen banana

1/2 cup frozen berries (raspberry or blueberry)

1/4 cup frozen tropical fruit - mango and papaya

1/3 to 1/2 cup frozen chopped spinach

1-2 scoops protein powder

Water as needed

1. Add all to a blender

2. Blend until smooth, adding water or ice if necessary.

PANCAKES AND WAFFLES

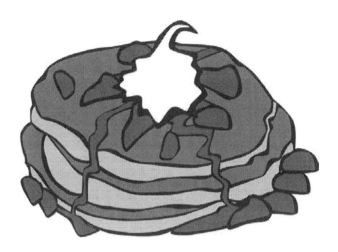

PANCAKE MASTER MIX

10 cups flour (use a GF mix and 5 tsp. Xanthan Gum)

2-1/2 cups instant powdered milk

1/2 cup sugar

1/4 cup Baking Powder

2 Tbs. salt

1. Mix the above and store in an air-tight container.

2. _To Make 8 Pancakes:_ Mix 1-1/2 cups of the master mix, 1 egg, 1 cup water, and 3 Tbs. oil.

3. Cook on a greased hot griddle.

46

PUMPKIN PANCAKES

2 cups biscuit mix (use GF Bisquick mix)

2 Tbs. packed brown sugar

2 tsp. cinnamon

1 tsp. allspice

1-1/2 cups (12 ounces) undiluted canned milk

1/2 cup solid pumpkin

2 Tbs. oil

2 eggs

1 tsp. vanilla

1. In a large bowl, combine biscuit mix, cinnamon, allspice, and sugar.

2. Add milk, pumpkin, eggs, oil, and vanilla; beat until smooth.

3. Pour 1/4 to 1/3 cup batter on a greased griddle and cook. Makes 16 pancakes

YUMMY BLENDER WHEAT PANCAKES

These can't be made Gluten Free

1-1/2 cups buttermilk

3/4 cup whole wheat kernels

3 heaping Tbs. cornmeal

1 heaping Tbs. brown sugar

2 eggs

1/4 cup butter; cut in small pieces

1 heaping Tbs. Rumford brand baking powder

1/4 to 1/2 tsp. baking soda

1. Liquefy in blender for 4 minutes: 1-1/2 cups buttermilk and 3/4 cup whole wheat kernels

2. Add: 3 Tbs. corn meal (heaping), 1 Tbs. heaping brown sugar, 2 eggs, and 1/4 cup butter; cut in small pieces and liquefy for 30 seconds.

3. Add: 1 Tbs. Rumford brand baking powder (heaping) and 1/4 – 1/2 tsp. soda

4. Switch blender on and off again to just blend in baking powder. Let rise to the top of blender before pouring onto a hot greased griddle. Cook and enjoy!

OVEN-BAKED BLUEBERRY PANCAKE

1 cup flour (Gluten Free flour mix and 1/2 tsp. xanthan gum)

3 Tbs. plus 1 tsp. sugar

1-1/2 tsp. baking powder

1/2 tsp. salt

3/4 cup whole milk

1 large egg, room temperature

2 Tbs. unsalted butter, melted, plus 1 Tbs. for pan

1 cup blueberries

Maple syrup for serving

1. Preheat oven to 375 degrees with the rack in the upper third. Place a 10-inch cast-iron skillet or other ovenproof skillet inside to heat up.

2. Whisk flour (gluten flour mix and 1/2 tsp. xanthan gum), 3 Tbs. sugar, baking powder, and salt. Also whisk together the milk, egg, and melted butter. Add the two together and mix until just combined.

3. Remove skillet from oven and add 1 Tbs. butter to coat. Pour in the pancake batter, and smooth top with an offset spatula. Sprinkle on blueberries and 1 tsp. sugar.

4. Bake until golden and cooked through, about 25 minutes. Remove from oven and cool for 5 minutes before dusting with powdered sugar and serving with syrup. Serves 4

CHUNKY MONKEY PANCAKES

1-1/2 cups flour (GF mix & 3/4 tsp. Xanthan)

3 Tbs. sugar

2 tsp. baking powder

1-1/2 tsp. baking soda

1/4 tsp. salt

1-1/2 cups buttermilk

1 large egg

1 Tbs. oil

1 tsp. vanilla

2 small bananas, mashed

6 Tbs. mini chocolate chips or regular ones, roughly chopped

Cooking spray or butter for pan

1. Combine dry ingredients with a whisk. Mix wet ingredients in a separate bowl. Add wet to dry and mix until just moistened. Fold in bananas and chocolate chips.

2. Heat griddle and coat it with cooking spray or butter. Use 1/4 cup batter per pancake. Wait for bubbles to form and then flip. Serve with warm Maple Peanut Butter Syrup below.

MAPLE PEANUT-BUTTER SYRUP

1/2 cup peanut butter

1 cup 100% real maple syrup

1. Heat 1/2 cup peanut butter in microwave for 30 seconds.

2. Add 1 cup 100% real maple syrup; microwave for another 30 seconds to warm.

3. Great over pancakes!

GERMAN PANCAKES

1/2 cup milk

1/2 cup flour (GF mix & 1/4 tsp. Xanthan)

3 large eggs

Dash salt

2 Tbs. butter

Raspberries, strawberries, bananas, pineapple or blueberries, to your taste

Brown sugar

Whipped cream or sour cream to top the fruit –use what you like best

1. Put the milk, flour, eggs, and salt in mixing bowl; mix with whisk.

2. Melt 1 tablespoon butter in each of two 9-inch pie plates in a preheated 425 degree oven. Butter should be sizzling. Swish butter around to grease bottom.

3. Pour batter into pie plate until 1/4–inch thick.

4. Bake 10-15 minutes until golden brown. Edges will puff up. Pancake will form a well in the center.

5. Spoon the fruit into the center, sprinkle with brown sugar and top with either whipped cream or sour cream. Serves 4

CORN CAKES

2 cups cornmeal

1/2 tsp. salt

2 Tbs. sugar

2 Tbs. baking powder

1 tsp. baking soda

2 eggs, beaten

1-1/2 cups buttermilk

1/4 cup melted butter, cooled to warm

1. Mix together the dry ingredients. Mix wet ingredients. Blend wet with dry.

2. Heat a griddle and lightly oil. Pour 1/4 cup mix onto griddle. Cook until bubbles form on top and then flip and cook the other side.

3. Serve with maple syrup and butter.

THE BEST GLUTEN FREE PANCAKES

2 cups Featherlight mix (in the of GF Substitutions Section) or regular flour

1 tsp. xanthan gum (use for GF only--don't use for regular wheat pancakes)

5 tsp. baking powder

1/2 tsp. salt

2-1/2 Tbs. sugar

2 cups milk

5 Tbs. oil

2 eggs

1. Mix dry ingredients in a large bowl. Mix wet ingredients in a medium bowl. Add wet to dry and mix well.

2. Cook on a warm griddle until bubbles appear; flip and cook other side. Serve with syrup.

THE BEST GLUTEN FREE WAFFLES

These also freeze well...just pop into the toaster or microwave to heat.

3 eggs, separated

1/4 cup sugar, scant

1-3/4 cup milk

1/2 cup oil

1 tsp. xanthan gum (GF only)

2 cups Featherlight mix (or reg. flour)

1/2 tsp. salt

1 Tbs. baking powder

1. Beat egg whites until foamy. Slowly add sugar and continue beating until whites form soft peaks.

2. In a different bowl, combine Featherlight mix, xanthan gum, salt and baking powder. Add egg yolks, milk and oil and stir.

3. Fold this batter into the egg whites, being careful not to deflate too much.

4. Bake on a hot waffle iron. Keep waffles in a warm oven (with door cracked open) until ready to eat.

PERFECT DAIRY FREE AND GLUTEN FREE ALMOND FLOUR PANCAKES

Nicholeen Peck

1-1/2 cups fine ground blanched almond flour - scoop into cup and level—don't pack

1/2 tsp. baking soda

1/4 tsp. salt

1/2 tsp. cinnamon (optional)

3 large eggs

4-5 Tbs. full fat coconut milk or as needed for consistency

2 Tbs. honey

1 tsp. vanilla or juice of half a lemon

Oil for frying

1/4 cup fruit, optional—to add to the batter (like blueberries etc.)

1. In a medium bowl, whisk the almond flour, baking soda, salt and cinnamon.

2. In another bowl, mix egg, coconut milk, honey and vanilla. Add liquid ingredients to dry ingredients along with optional fruit and mix well. Let batter rest for a few minutes.

3. Preheat griddle over medium heat (or cast iron skillet). Pancakes will burn if heat is too hot and also hard to turn over. Batter should sizzle when it hits the pan.

4. Fry pancake and flip when it starts to bubble and edges dry. Smaller pancakes are easier to flip.

5. Continue to cook until they puff and firm up. This makes about 25-30 dollar-size pancakes. These freeze well.

6. Top with honey, pure maple syrup, or cold coconut cream.

BLENDER GLUTEN FREE OAT PANCAKES

2 cups milk

1-1/3 c. whole oats- use oat groats if available (use GF)

2 eggs

3/4 c. oil

2 Tbs. sugar

1 tsp. baking soda

1 tsp. baking powder

1 tsp. salt

1/4 tsp. xanthan gum

1. Place oats and milk in a blender. Blend on medium high speed for 4 minutes.

2. Add the rest of the ingredients and blend on high speed until combined.

3. Bake on a 350 degree greased griddle. Serve with Berry Syrup (recipe p. 59) and whipped cream or cool whip.

NOTE:
- ✓ *I have used gluten free rolled oats instead of whole oats, but the texture wasn't quite the same. They baked differently. I'm going to keep experimenting, though, because the GF rolled oats are much easier to find than the whole oats.*

BUCKWHEAT PANCAKES

Makes about 8 pancakes

1 cup buckwheat flour (this flour is naturally GF)

1 teaspoon baking powder

2 tablespoons sugar or honey

1/2 teaspoon salt

1 egg, beaten

1 cup milk or buttermilk

2 tablespoons melted butter

1. Preheat griddle or skillet (if electric, go about 375 degrees). Lightly grease griddle.

2. In a bowl, place all dry ingredients, mix together. Make a well in the bottom of the bowl.

3. In a smaller bowl, mix wet ingredients together. Add this in the middle of the well you just created and mix until blended.

4. Make your pancakes by using 1/4 cup batter for each one and cook on the griddle. Enjoy with a little butter and real maple syrup for an amazing treat!

FRENCH TOAST

FRENCH TOAST

Serves 4

4 eggs

1 teaspoon sugar, optional

Dash salt

1 cup milk

10 to 12 slices white bread (use GF bread)

Butter or oil for skillet or griddle

1/4 t. vanilla

1/4 tsp. cinnamon, if desired, for cinnamon French toast

Maple syrup or other syrup

1. Break eggs into a wide, shallow bowl or pie plate; beat lightly with a fork. Stir in sugar, salt, vanilla, cinnamon and milk.

2. Over medium-low heat, heat griddle or skillet coated with a thin layer of butter or oil.

3. Place the bread slices, one at a time, into the bowl or plate, letting the slices soak up egg mixture for a few seconds, then carefully turn to coat the other side. Soak/coat only as many slices as you will be cooking at one time.

4. Transfer bread slices to griddle or skillet, cooking slowly until bottom is golden brown. Turn and brown the other side. Serve French toast hot with butter and syrup.

MAKE AHEAD (OVERNIGHT) FRENCH TOAST CASSEROLE

8 large eggs

2-1/4 cups half and half or whole milk

1/4 cup sugar

1/4 cup brown sugar

1-1/2 tsp. vanilla

1-1/2 tsp. cinnamon

1 (12-16 ounce) loaf French bread-cubed (use GF bread)

1 8-ounce pkg. cream cheese; cut into small pieces

1. Coat a 9x13 baking dish with non-stick spray or butter.

2. In a bowl, mix together all ingredients down to the bread.

3. Arrange half of bread cubes in pan and pour 1/2 of egg mixture and all cream cheese cubes.

4. Top with remaining bread and egg mixture. Cover with foil. Refrigerate overnight.

5. Bake 350 for 55-60 minutes. Dust on powdered sugar. Serve with butter & syrup.

FRENCH TOAST CASSEROLE

One 10-oz loaf French bread; cut into 1-in cubes (use GF bread)

8 eggs

3 cups milk

4 tsp. sugar

1 tsp. vanilla

3/4 tsp. salt

Maple syrup-optional

Topping:

2 Tbs. butter, cubed

3 Tbs. sugar

2 tsp. cinnamon

1. Place bread cubes in a greased 9 x 13-inch baking dish. In a mixing bowl, beat eggs, milk, sugar, vanilla and salt. Pour over the bread.

2. Cover and refrigerate 8 hours or overnight. Remove 30 minutes before baking the next morning and dot with the butter. Combine cinnamon and sugar; sprinkle over the top.

3. Cover and bake at 350 degrees for 45-50 minutes or until a knife inserted near the center comes out clean. Let stand for 5 minutes. Serve with maple syrup, if desired.

CREPES

CREPES

1 cup all-purpose flour

2 teaspoons sugar

1/4 teaspoon salt

1 cup low-fat 1% milk

1/2 cup water

2 teaspoons butter, melted

2 large eggs

1. Lightly spoon flour into a dry measuring cup; level with a knife. Combine flour, sugar, and salt in a small bowl. Combine milk, water, melted butter, and eggs in a blender. Add the flour mixture to milk mixture, and process until smooth. Cover batter; chill for 1 hour.

2. Heat an 8-inch nonstick crepe pan or skillet over medium heat. Pour a scant 1/4 cup batter into pan; quickly tilt pan in all directions so batter covers pan with a thin film. Cook about 1 minute. Carefully lift the edge of the crepe with a spatula to test for doneness. The crepe is ready to turn when it can be shaken loose from the pan and the underside is lightly browned. Turn crepe over, and cook for 30 seconds or until center is set.

3. Place crepe on a towel; cool completely. Repeat procedure with the remaining batter, stirring batter between crepes. Stack crepes between single layers of wax paper to prevent sticking.

CREPES – GLUTEN FREE

Travis and Annmarie

3 cups milk

6 eggs

1 Tbs. melted butter or oil

1 tsp. salt

1/2 tsp. xanthan gum (use only for GF)

1 cup GF Featherlight mix (or white flour)

1/2 cup GF mix (or white flour)

1. In a large bowl, beat milk, eggs, and melted butter until smooth. Slowly add salt, xanthan gum and flours. Mix until the batter is the consistency of heavy cream.

2. Heat a 6-inch crepe pan or a non-stick frying pan on medium heat. (If your pan is older, it sometimes helps to spray it with non-stick cooking spray.) Spoon 2 to 4 tablespoons of batter into the bottom of the pan. Move pan from side to side to coat bottom.

3. Brown the crepe on one side and then flip with a spatula and brown the other side. Keep warm in the oven. Serve with your favorite toppings: fruit, cream, Lemon Curd, Nutella, etc.

4. These can be frozen to use later if layered between sheets of parchment paper. Thaw overnight in the refrigerator. This makes approximately 15 crepes.

5. *More Topping Ideas:* whipped cream, any fresh fruit, cinnamon and sugar, syrup, butter, chicken, sausage and eggs, tomatoes and bacon, powdered sugar, hard boiled eggs, cream cheese and jam. Great served with Nutella, fresh fruit or preserves, or even savory fillings.

TOP IT OFF WITH BUTTER AND SYRUP

BERRY SYRUP

2 cups frozen berries (I use a Triple Berry Blend)

1 Tbs. lemon juice

2 Tbs. water

Tbs. sugar

1 dash cinnamon

1. Combine all ingredients in a small saucepan. Bring to a boil over medium high heat, stirring occasionally.

2. Remove from heat. Blend with a stick blender or regular blender.

PUMPKIN SAUCE FOR PANCAKES OR WAFFLES

Annette Vandersteen

1-1/2 cups canned pumpkin

3/4 cup sugar

3/4 tsp. cinnamon

1/8 tsp. nutmeg

1/8 tsp. cloves

1/2 cup milk

1/2 tsp. salt

1/3 cup raisins - optional

1. Mix and cook until warm.

2. Serve over waffles or pancakes.

CINNAMON SYRUP

Jessica Davenport   Crowd Pleaser!

1/2 cup white corn syrup

1 cup sugar

1/4 cup water

1 tsp. cinnamon

1/2 cup evaporated canned milk

1. In a saucepan, add the corn syrup, sugar, water, and cinnamon. Bring to boil, while stirring constantly. Cook 2 minutes after it boils.

2. Remove from heat, cool 5 minutes and then stir in 1/2 cup evaporated milk. Enjoy!

HOMEMADE MAPLE SYRUP WITH BUTTER FLAVOR

4 cups sugar or 2 cups white sugar and 2 cups brown sugar

2 cups water

1/2 cup white corn syrup

1 Tbs. maple flavoring

1 tsp. vanilla

1 tsp. butter flavor (optional)

1. Bring all to a boil to melt the sugar.

2. Enjoy!

MAPLE PEANUT-BUTTER SYRUP

1/2 cup peanut butter

1 cup 100% pure maple syrup

1. Heat 1/2 cup peanut butter in microwave for 30 seconds; add 1 cup 100% real maple syrup.

2. Microwave for another 30 seconds to warm. Great over pancakes!

PEACH OR APRICOT SYRUP FOR PANCAKES ETC.

1 -1/4 cups fresh peach or apricot puree

1-3/4 cups sugar

1. Boil 1 minute and then put in pints and process 10 minutes

2. If you don't wish to bottle this, just cook and use. Canned fruit can also be used, just cut down on the sugar. Keep refrigerated after use.

HONEY BUTTER

1/2 cup butter, softened

1/4 tsp. vanilla

1/2 cup honey

1. Whip butter. Add vanilla and honey gradually.

2. Beat for 2 minutes. Makes 1 cup

HONEY BUTTER -- #2

One can also add 1-2 tsp. cinnamon for a variation or 1 tsp. vanilla

1 cup butter

2/3 cup honey

3/4 cup powdered sugar

1. Beat butter, honey and powdered sugar until light and fluffy

2. Do this for about 30 seconds.

RASPBERRY BUTTER

Great for toast, scones, or pancakes...

1/2 cup softened butter

1/4 cup raspberry preserves

1/4 cup fresh raspberries

1 Tbs. powdered sugar

1. Beat the butter, raspberries and powdered sugar together in a bowl until well combined.

2. Refrigerate until set; about 1 hour

BREADS, GF BREADS, ROLLS, MUFFINS, & QUICK BREADS

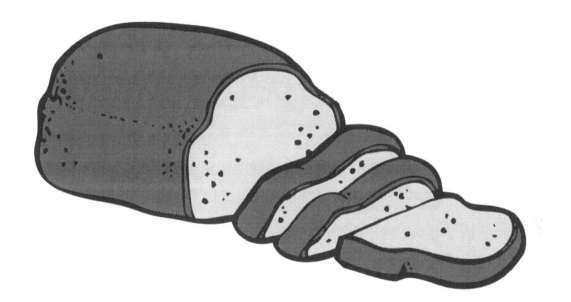

BREADS AND ROLLS...

JANEEN'S BASIC WHITE BREAD

(5 medium loaves) - This can't be made Gluten Free!

5 cups warm water

1/2 cup sugar

2 Tbs. yeast

2 Tbs. salt

1-1/2 cups white flour

1 cup instant powdered milk - optional

1/2 cup oil

9 to 12 cups of white flour

Shortening to grease the loaf pans

1. In the Bosch mixing bowl or other large bowl, mix together and let sit until the yeast bubbles: 5 cups warm water, 1/2 cup sugar, and 2 Tbs. yeast.

2. Mix in after the yeast bubbles: 2 Tbs. salt, 1-1/2 cups flour, 1 cup powdered milk (opt.) and 1/2 cup oil.

3. With the Bosch mixer running, add flour to mixture (about 9--12 cups) until the dough just leaves and cleans the side of the Bosch bowl or if doing this by hand, the dough is stiff enough to knead without being too sticky.

4. Knead for 5 minutes with Bosch or 10 minutes by hand on a flour dusted counter. Remove the dough hook from the Bosch. Cover the bowl and let rise until double in size--about 45 minutes. Punch down.

5. Form into 5 loaves and put into greased loaf pans, cover, and let rise until double.

6. Bake 375 degrees for 25-30 minutes until top sounds hollow when tapped. Remove from pans onto a clean linen dish cloth and cool on their side. Enjoy!

7. ***For Scones***: Let dough rise the first time in a covered greased bowl. Heat some oil in a skillet. Pull off small pieces of the dough, stretch to shape, and fry until done. Don't fry on too high of heat or else they will be doughy in the middle. ·

8. I have also made ***Pizza Crusts*** with the dough. I spread dough out on a greased pizza pan(s) and bake for 10 minutes to prebake it and stop the yeast from raising anymore....let it cool and freeze until needed. Take out of freezer, load with sauce and toppings and bake at 400 degrees until cheese melts....Enjoy!

To Make Dinner Rolls: In greased muffin tins, place some dough in each section. Freeze until firm. Either place in a ziploc bag until needed or cover dough in the muffin tins.

To Serve Rolls: Remove from freezer and let thaw in muffin tins until double in bulk or place individual frozen rolls in a greased baking dish and let rise until double in bulk. Bake at 350 degrees 12 to 15 minutes or until browned and done--might take longer for a baking dish.

FOOLPROOF WHOLE WHEAT BREAD - (BOSCH)

This bread can't be made Gluten Free!

Small Batch	Regular Batch	
4	6	cups warm water
1	1-1/2	Tbs. salt
1/3	1/2	cup oil
1/3	1/2	cup honey
1-1/2	2	Tbs. dough enhancer
2	3	Tbs. Instant Saf brand yeast
7	10	cups wheat kernels
4	6	4 x 8-inch bread pans

1. Freshly grind wheat on medium setting in a wheat grinder; set aside.

2. Add water and several cups of freshly ground flour to Bosch mixing bowl with dough hook in place. Mix with a few short bursts of the jog switch.

3. Add salt, honey, oil, dough enhancer, instant yeast, and jog briefly. (If the quality of your wheat is maybe low in gluten, add 3-4 Tbsp. gluten powder, also.)

4. While the Bosch is kneading at speed 1, slowly add whole wheat flour until dough pulls away from and cleans side of mixing bowl. This normally will normally take most of the whole wheat flour you have ground. It is better to add too little flour than too much. Allow the Bosch to knead the dough until the gluten is properly developed--about 10-12 minutes.

5. Turn oven on to pre-heat to 150 Degrees. Shape into loaves and place in well-greased pans. Turn oven off and then place loaves into the oven and raise until double in bulk - about 25 minutes.

6. When loaves are double in size, set the oven to 350 degrees and turn it on (leave loaves in oven). Bake 30-35 minutes.

7. When loaves are done, immediately remove from pans and let cool on wire rack. (Hint: So pans won't stick the next time you bake bread, wipe out while hot and don't wash them.)

BERNICE GUNDRY'S POTATO ROLLS

Makes about 3-1/2 dozen rolls --- Can't be made GF

1 yeast cake or 1 Tbs. dry yeast

1/2 cup warm water

1 tsp. sugar

2/3 cup oil

1 tsp. salt

1/4 cup sugar

1 cup (about 2) mashed potatoes (no lumps) - instant potatoes can be used

1 cup milk, scalded and cooled

2 beaten eggs

5 to 7 cups flour or more

Butter, melted for the insides and tops of rolls

1. Put 1 yeast cake or 1 Tbs. dry yeast in 1/2 cup warm water with 1 tsp. sugar and let it dissolve.

2. Put the following in Bosch Mixer bowl or other large mixing bowl: 2/3 cup oil, 1 tsp. salt, and 1/4 cup sugar, 1 cup (about 2) mashed potatoes (no lumps), 1 cup milk, scalded and cooled (Heat until scum forms on top, no hotter), and 2 beaten eggs.

3. Mix together and add 2-3 cups of white flour. Mix again and add yeast that has become bubbly and risen. Add 3-4 more cups of flour until a medium stiff dough forms. Mix it in well. If you do not have a Bosch mixer you will have to oil your hands and mix the last flour in with your hands.

4. Place in an oiled bowl covered with plastic wrap and let raise double in bulk. Punch down and either shape into desired rolls or rub top with butter and cover with plastic wrap and put into refrigerator until ready to shape rolls.

5. Bernice used an oiled surface to roll out dough & cut into rolls. Raise rolls until double.

6. Bake 10-15 minutes in a 350 degree oven on a greased, oiled, or sprayed sheet pans. A little melted butter can be put on top of each roll before baking.

<u>NOTE:</u>
✓ *This recipe can be shaped after rising double in bulk or it can be refrigerated (even overnight) before shaping the rolls. You can also double or triple the recipe.*

SUGGESTION:
- ✓ *This can also be used for **Cinnamon Rolls.** See Annette's version below. After the first rising, roll into a rectangle, spread with melted butter, cinnamon and sugar etc. Roll up and cut with dental floss into slices. Place on greased cookie sheet. Raise 30 minutes or so. Bake 350 degrees about 15-20 minutes. Frost them after cooling with your favorite frosting.*

ANNETTE'S CINNAMON ROLLS AND FROSTING

1 recipe of Bernice's Potato Rolls - recipe above

Melted butter

Cinnamon

Sugar

Frosting of your choice

1. Annette makes the potato rolls above. After they have doubled in bulk, roll out into a rectangle about 1/2-inch thick.

2. Spread on melted butter and sprinkle with cinnamon-sugar (heavy on the cinnamon).

3. Roll up into a log shape and cut into 1-inch thick slices with a piece of dental floss.

4. Lay on a greased baking sheet. Cover and let rise until double.

5. Bake at 375 degrees for 15 minutes or until golden brown. Remove and cool.

6. Frost them with the Cream Cheese Frosting below or icing of your choice.

CREAM CHEESE FROSTING

4 ounces cream cheese

1/2 cup butter

1 tsp. vanilla

Dash of almond extract

3 cups plus powdered sugar

Splash of milk

1. Cream 4 oz. cream cheese and 1/2 cup butter; add 1 tsp. vanilla and if desired, a touch of almond extract.

2. Mix in powdered sugar and a bit of milk until consistency to spread on the cinnamon rolls.

3. Frost the rolls.

ANNETTE'S ORANGE ROLLS

1 recipe of Bernice's Potato rolls above

Melted butter

1/3 cup soft butter

1/2 cup sugar

Zest of 1 orange

Frosting:

Juice of 1 orange

Powdered sugar

1. Make Bernice's potato rolls (page 66) and let raise double. Roll out into a rectangle.

2. Spread on melted butter and roll up into a log, cut into 1-inch slices, and place on greased baking sheet.

3. Brush the top of each roll with a mixture of: 1/3 cup really soft butter, 1/2 cup sugar and the zest of 1 orange.

4. Let rise and bake at 400 degrees for 12 to 15 minutes.

5. Frost with a glaze of powdered sugar mixed with the juice of an orange.

JANEEN'S CINNAMON CHRISTMAS TREES

Makes 2 large or 4 small trees--Can't be GF! We have these every Christmas Morning Breakfast with our Breakfast Casserole and Orange juice!

2 Tbs. yeast

1 cup milk; scalded and cooled (or add 1/4 cup powdered milk to warm water)

2 eggs

1 tsp. salt

1/2 cup sugar

1/4 cup shortening

4 cups flour

Melted butter

Cinnamon

Sugar

Green sugar

Colored sprinkles

Frosting - green or white

Walnut/Pecan halves

1. Dissolve: 2 Tbs. dry yeast in 1 cup of scalded and cooled milk – or use 1/4 cup powdered milk in warm water

2. Add: 2 eggs, 1 tsp. salt, 1/2 cup sugar, 1/4 cup shortening, 4 cups of flour and mix well. Turn out on a floured board and knead until smooth and elastic. Cover and let rise until double. Divide dough into 2 pieces or sections.

3. To Form The Trees:

4. Roll each of the sections into approximately a 14" circle. Brush with melted butter and sprinkle with cinnamon and sugar.

5. Fold sides of circle in at top forming a point leaving a half circle at the bottom (the trunk).

6. Cut with scissors the half circle in about 4 inches on each side. Roll one side in like a cinnamon roll and then roll the other side around it to form the trunk.

7. Cut the folded sides (that forms the point) in about 2-3 inches on both sides. Cut the strips (these are making the branches) about 1 inch wide and line up cuts evenly on both sides.

8. Fold each of these strips up and over to show the cinnamon roll inside.

9. Brush all over with melted butter. Put walnut halves up the center of tree. Let rise.

10. Bake at 350 for 18-20 minutes. While still warm, drizzle icing made of powdered sugar, milk, and vanilla over the tree (could also make a cream cheese frosting- p.69). Sprinkle with green sugar over the tree and also some colored sprinkles to look like lights etc.

OPTIONAL ALMOND FILLING:

- ✓ *Mix 1/4 cup butter, 3/4 cup sugar, 2 tsp. almond extract, and 1/3 cup quick oats that have been blended in the blender. Use this in place of the cinnamon sugar.*

"EASY" NO RISE CINNAMON ROLLS

Gluten Free changes in Parenthesis

4 cups Bisquick mix - (GF use 1 box (about 3 cups) Gluten Free Bisquick Mix)

1-1/4 cup buttermilk - (GF use 1 cup or enough for the dough to stick together)

4 Tbs. sugar - (GF 3 Tbs.)

Extra flour (use GF mix) for rolling out dough

1 cup brown sugar - (GF use 3/4 cup)

1/4 cup granulated sugar - (GF use 3 Tbs.)

1 Tbs. of cinnamon - (GF use 2-1/2 tsp.)

1/2 cup chopped nuts (I used pecans)

2 Tablespoons butter melted - (GF use 1 ½ Tbs.)

3/4 cup butter, melted and cooled - (GF use 1/2 cup)

1 cup powdered sugar - (GF use 3/4 cup)

1-2 Tablespoons milk - (GF use 1-2 Tbs.)

1 tsp. of vanilla - (GF use 3/4 tsp.)

1. In a large bowl, combine Bisquick, buttermilk and sugar in a bowl using a fork. Mix just until all combined to create a dough.

2. In a medium bowl, combine brown sugar, granulated sugar, cinnamon and nuts in separate bowl. Add 2 tablespoons melted butter and stir to moisten. Set aside.

3. Generously flour rolling surface. I roll on parchment paper for GF. This is a sticky dough. Turn dough out onto surface and start patting into a rectangular shape with your hand. Flour your hand well also.

4. Use a rolling pin to thin dough to about 1/2 inch thickness. Do not over-roll, the dough will stick.

5. Once rolled out, pour 3/4 cup melted butter over entire surface then spread with pastry brush to even out and get to the edges.

6. Sprinkle sugar/nut mixture over butter. Start rolling dough from long end.

7. Slice into 1 inch to 1/2 inch slices. I used dental floss to slice mine. It really does work, without mushing the pastry.

8. Transfer slices to a well-greased (sprayed) 9 x 13 pan. I used a spatula to make it easier.

9. Bake in preheated 375 degree oven for 25-30 minutes, until just golden brown on tops.

10. Combine powdered sugar, milk and vanilla until desired consistency and drizzle over topped of rolls. Let cinnamon rolls sit for 5 minutes before serving.

RASPBERRY BUTTER

Great for toast, scones, or pancakes...

1/2 cup softened butter

1/4 cup raspberry preserves

1/4 cup fresh raspberries

1 Tbs. powdered sugar

1. Beat the butter, raspberries and powdered sugar together in a bowl until well combined.

2. Refrigerate until set; about 1 hour

HONEY BUTTER

1/2 cup butter, softened

1/4 tsp. vanilla

1/2 cup honey

1. Whip butter. Add vanilla and honey gradually.

2. Beat for 2 minutes. Makes 1 cup

HONEY BUTTER -- #2

One can also add 1-2 tsp. cinnamon for a variation or 1 tsp. vanilla

1 cup butter

2/3 cup honey

3/4 cup powdered sugar

1. Beat butter, honey and powdered sugar until light and fluffy

2. For about 30 seconds.

FRESH HERB BUTTER

This herb butter enhances the flavors of grilled seafood, chicken, or steak. Try adding to rice, pasta, and soups. For the most flavor, mash in as much of the herbs as the butter will hold. Any tender herb is appropriate. Wrap tightly in plastic so it doesn't absorb odors.

1 lb. unsalted butter, cut into pieces and softened to room temperature

Salt and freshly ground pepper to taste

1/4 cup lemon juice

4 cups assorted fresh tender herb leaves, chopped (tarragon, thyme, parsley, basil, dill, chives, marjoram, chervil, oregano, mint etc. Use what sounds good to you.)

1. In a food processor, combine butter, salt and pepper. Process this until you get a creamy paste, scraping down the sides as necessary.

2. Add lemon juice and process until creamy. Add herb leaves and process again until well blended.

3. Shape into two logs on parchment or wax paper. Roll tightly and wrap well in plastic. Chill or freeze (up to 3 months).

4. Slice off a slice and lay it on the hot food just before serving.

VARIATIONS:
- ✓ *Add 1 clove minced garlic to 1/2 cup of this mix for garlic-herb butter.*
- ✓ *Lemon juice can be left out if only using for herb butter on breads, etc.*

GLUTEN FREE BREADS AND ROLLS...

GLUTEN-FREE BREAD FLOUR MIX - MIX A

1/3 part millet flour	2 cups	1 cup
1/6 part sorghum flour	1 cup	1/2 cup
1/6 part cornstarch	1 cup	1/2 cup
1/6 part potato starch	1 cup	1/2 cup
1/6 part tapioca flour/starch	1 cup	1/2 cup
Total	6 cups	3 cups (For 1 loaf of bread)

GLUTEN FREE BREAD FLOUR - MIX B

1/4 part millet flour	1-1/2 cups	1/2 cup	1/3 cup plus 1 Tbs.
1/4 part sorghum flour	1-1/2 cups	1/2 cup	1/3 cup plus 1 Tbs.
1/6 part cornstarch	1 cup	1/3 cup	1/4 cup
1/6 part potato starch	1 cup	1/3 cup	1/4 cup
1/6 part tapioca flour	1 cup	1/3 cup	1/4 cup
Total:	6 cups	2 cups	1-1/2 cups

74

TAPIOCA BREAD (GLUTEN FREE)

Our Favorite Gluten Free Bread!

1 Tbs. dry yeast granules

1/2 cup lukewarm water

2 cups rice flour

1-1/2 cups tapioca starch (flour)

1/4 cup sugar

2 tsp. sugar

2-1/2 tsp. xanthan gum

1/4 cup shortening

1/2 cup dry instant powdered Milk or Dairy Free instant

1-1/4 cup hot water

3/4 tsp. salt

1 tsp. dough enhancer or vinegar

1 egg plus 2 egg whites (or 3/4 c. liquid eggs)

1. Grease 2 (8 ½" x 4 1/2 ") loaf pans and dust with rice flour.

2. Combine flours, sugar, xanthan gum, milk powder and salt in the large bowl of the Bosch mixer or other mixer.

3. In a separate bowl, sprinkle yeast into lukewarm water with 2 tsp. sugar and let dissolve.

4. Melt shortening in 1-1/4 cups of hot water. (put this in microwave for 30 seconds to warm)

5. Pour shortening mixture and vinegar or dough enhancer into dry ingredients and blend on low. Add eggs and beat for a few seconds. Add yeast mixture and beat on high for 3-1/2 minutes.

6. Spoon the dough into prepared greased pans. Let dough rise until doubled in bulk (35-40 minutes for rapid rise yeast and 50-60 for regular yeast).

7. Bake in a preheated 400 degree oven for 50-60 minutes. Cover with foil after the first 10 minutes of cooking to prevent being too brown……..I have baked mine at 350 for 12 minutes and then 40 minutes and it's been okay….bread will sound hollow when tapped when done. Breads internal temperature should be 200 degrees to be done.

VARIATIONS

- ✓ *I have also made **<u>Pizza Crusts</u>** with the dough. I spread dough out on a greased pizza pan(s) and bake for 10 minutes to prebake it and stop the yeast from raising anymore....let it cool and freeze until needed. Take out of freezer, load with sauce and toppings and bake at 400 degrees until cheese melts....Enjoy!*

- ✓ **<u>To Make Dinner Rolls</u>***: In greased muffin tins, place some dough in each section. Freeze until firm. Either place in a ziploc bag until needed or cover dough in the muffin tins.*

- ✓ **<u>To Serve Rolls:</u>** *Remove from freezer and let thaw in muffin tins until double in bulk or place individual frozen rolls in a greased baking dish and let rise until double in bulk. Bake at 350 degrees 12 to 15 minutes or until browned and done--might take longer for a baking dish.*

- ✓ **<u>For Scones</u>***: Let dough rise the first time in a covered greased bowl. Heat some oil in a skillet. Pull off small pieces of the dough, stretch to shape, and fry until done. Don't fry on too high of heat or else they will be doughy in the middle.*

BASIC SANDWICH BREAD - FOR THE BREAD MACHINE

I have a Cuisinart

1-1/4 cups milk (between 65 and 75 degrees - put in for 1 minute in microwave)

1/4 cup canola oil (between 65 and 75 degrees)

2 large eggs, room temperature (if cold put in bowl of hot water to warm)

3 cups Bread Flour Mix A, p. 73

3 Tablespoons sugar

2 1/4 teaspoons xanthan gum

3/4 teaspoon salt

1 packet (1/4 ounce) active dry yeast -- I use a rounded Tablespoon

1. Set machine to #5 -gluten free cycle --crust and size will be set automatically

2. Remove bread pan from machine and put kneading blade in securely.

3. Whisk milk, oil, and eggs with whisk until frothy (bubbles at top) in glass measuring cup and then pour in bread pan.

4. Wisk Bread Flour Mix A, sugar, xanthan gum, salt and yeast in small bowl and sprinkle over the liquids. Without pressing down excessively hard, try to spread out the dry ingredients so they cover all the liquid.

5. Put the bread pan in machine, and turn to right to secure it and close td. Press START....

6. Optional, but suggested.....while the bread is kneading scrape the sides with a rubber scraper if flour clings to sides.

7. Remove bread pan from machine when the BAKE cycle ends. Turn bread pan over to remove bread and place on rack to cool (use a rubber spatula to release it if it sticks so as not to scrape the non-stick pan). Bread should have a hollow sound when tapped on bottom and sides. Instant-read thermometer should register about 205 degrees

8. Store in refrigerator for up to a week or freeze up to 3 weeks. This can be cut into 16 slices.

GLUTEN FREE SANDWICH BREAD

Makes a 1-lb. loaf

2 large eggs – room temperature

3 Tbs. canola oil

2 cups Bread Flour Mix A or B (can use 1-3/4 c. mix & 1/4 c. sweet rice flour for softer bread) p. 73

1-1/2 tsp. Xanthan gum

1/2 tsp. salt

1 tsp. unflavored gelatin

2 Tbs. sugar

1 packet of active-rise yeast (not quick rise) or 1 rounded Tablespoon

3/4 cup plus 2 Tbs. milk, heated to 110 degrees

1. Grease an 8 ½ x 4 ½ -inch loaf pan with cooking spray & dusted with rice flour.

2. Mix eggs and oil together and set aside.

3. Mix all dry ingredients in large bowl of an electric mixer. Quickly add the warm milk and egg and oil mixture; mix until just blended. Scrape bowl and then beat at high speed for 3 minutes.

4. Spoon into bread pan.   Cover with a light cloth and let rise in a warm place for 30-40 minutes or until dough just reaches 1/2 inch below top of pan. If you use a warm 80 degree oven to help the bread rise, and you only have one oven, you will have to pull the bread out before preheating the oven.

5. Place rack in center of oven and preheat to 400 degrees.

6. Bake bread in center of oven for 10 minutes; cover with aluminum foil and bake another 40-45 minutes. Your bread should have a hollow sound when tapped on sides and bottom and your instant-read thermometer should register 195-200 degrees. Remove from oven and turn out on the side to cool on a rack.

7. Wrap bread in plastic wrap and then foil and then store in refrigerator or freezer.

78

FRENCH - ITALIAN SANDWICH BREAD

Makes delicious sandwiches, grilled cheese, or Panini

1-1/2 cups water (room-temperature)

2 tsp. olive oil (room temperature)

3 cups Bread Flour Mix A, p. 73

3 Tbs. sugar

2 tsp. xanthan gum

1 tsp. salt

1 packet (1/4 ounce) active dry yeast granules (not quick rise) or 1 Tbs., rounded

1. Set Bread Machine to "HOME MADE- MEMORY 1." Press "Crust Control" until the arrow points to Dark. I have a Cuisinart and I just use gluten free setting.

2. Remove bread pan from machine and make sure kneading blades are firmly secured in place.

3. Whisk water and olive oil in measuring cup and pour into bread pan.

4. Whisk Bread Mix A, sugar, xanthan gum, salt, and yeast in a small bowl until well combined and sprinkle over the liquids. Without pressing down excessively hard, try to spread out the dry ingredients so they cover the liquid.

5. Put bread pan into the machine, secure it in place, and close the lid. Press Start/Restart.

6. Optional, But Suggested: During the kneading cycle, scrape the pan with a rubber spatula if flour clings to sides.

7. Remove bread pan from machine promptly when Bake cycle ends. Turn bread pan over to remove bread and place on a wire rack to cool. Bread should have a hollow sound when you tap on bottom and sides or 205 degrees on a thermometer. Store in refrigerator for up to 1 week or freezer for up to 10 days.

<u>NOTE:</u>
- ✓ *For wonderful Panini herb bread, add 2-3 Tbs. fresh chopped Rosemary (2-3 tsp. dry) when the machine beeps on Add cycle and also could add grated parmesan cheese and olives. Sprinkle cornmeal on top also after it has mixed in.*

FARMHOUSE GLUTEN FREE BUTTERMILK BREAD – BREAD MACHINE

3 large eggs, lightly beaten

1/4 cup oil

1-1/4 cup plus 1 Tbs. milk, warmed

4 Tbs. dry buttermilk powder

2 cups brown rice flour

1/2 cup potato starch

1/2 cup tapioca starch/flour

3-1/2 teaspoons xanthan gum

1/4 cup sugar

1-1/2 teaspoons salt

2-1/4 teaspoons active dry yeast

1. Mix the warmed 1-1/4 cup plus 1 Tbs. milk and the 4 Tbs. dry buttermilk powder and let it dissolve. Mix all liquid ingredients together and pour into bread machine.

2. Mix all dry ingredients, except yeast, together and spoon over top of liquid ingredients. Sprinkle yeast over dry ingredients, and avoid touching sides of the pan.

3. Set bread machine to gluten free setting or basic loaf, light and press start.

4. After the bread is done, do not remove bread from pan until any stay warm cycle is finished and bread has cooled down.

ARTISAN GLUTEN-FREE FLOUR MIX

3 CUP MIX	**12 CUP MIX**
1-1/4 cups brown rice flour	5 cups brown rice flour
3/4 cup sorghum flour	3 cups sorghum flour
2/3 cup cornstarch	2-2/3 cups cornstarch
1/4 cup potato starch	1 cup potato starch
1 Tbs. + 1 tsp. potato flour	1/4 cup + 4 tsp. potato flour
1 tsp. xanthan gum	1 Tbs. + 1 tsp. xanthan gum

1. Don't densely pack flour.

2. Spoon into the cup and level off.

3. Store the extra in the refrigerator.

ARTISAN BREAD-GLUTEN FREE

2-1/4 cups milk

2 Tbs. sugar

1-1/2 tsp. salt

1 Tbs. butter

3 cups artisan GF flour mix, p.80 above

1 cup sorghum flour

1 tsp. xanthan gum

2-1/4 tsp. yeast

1. Heat until butter is melted: 2-1/4 cup milk, 2 Tbs. sugar, 1-1/2 tsp. salt and 1 Tbs. butter

2. Mix the following dry ingredients together and then add milk mix above: 3 cups artisan GF flour mix, 1 cup sorghum flour, 1 tsp. xanthan gum, and 2-1/4 tsp. yeast

3. Mix on high for 3 minutes and then spread into a greased 9 x 5 loaf pan.

4. Cover and rise for 60 minutes. Bake at 375 degrees until done, about 30 to 40 min. Cool.

GLUTEN FREE WHITE SANDWICH BREAD OR ENGLISH MUFFINS

Though this bread doesn't dry out immediately, it keeps best when refrigerated or frozen. After baking, let the bread cool completely for at least an hour.

3 cups Bette Hagman's GF flour mix, p. 271

1-3/4 cup warm water

1/4 cup sugar

1/4 cup oil

3-1/2 teaspoons xanthan gum

1 tsp. rice vinegar

1-1/2 tsp. salt

3 eggs

1-1/2 Tablespoons yeast

1. Mix flour mix, sugar, xanthan gum and salt together in a bowl of a stand mixer. Dump yeast on top of dry ingredients, but don't mix in.

2. Combine water, oil, and vinegar in separate bowl. Pour on top of yeast and let sit 3 minutes. Mix together on low speed. Add eggs. Mix until combined and then beat on high speed for 5 minutes.

3. Grease 2 regular loaf pans (8x4x2) or 12 English muffin rings. Spoon bread into pans and let rise for about 20 minutes. As bread is rising, preheat oven to 375 degrees.

4. Bake loaf pans about 35 minutes. English muffin rings, rolls, or small loaves bake for 20-25 minutes. The bread will be deep brown in color when done. Remove and let cool.

5. Slice it and place into a zip-lock bag in fridge or freezer. When ready to use, place the desired number of slices on a plate and microwave on high for 20-30 seconds. It will taste as if you just pulled it from the oven.

6. *English muffin rings* can be bought at most kitchen stores. If you don't have them, fold 7x12 inch pieces of foil in half and then in thirds lengthwise, forming 6 layers in all. Bend in circles and secure with tape.

7. Wrap bread in plastic wrap and then foil and then store in refrigerator or freezer.

GLUTEN FREE TEMPURA BATTER

2 eggs

2 cups rice flour

2 cups club soda or sparkling water

1. Mix all and dip your choice of vegetables or shrimp into batter.

2. Fry at 375 degrees in peanut oil. Drain on paper towels

BRUSCHETTA/OR TOAST POINTS BREAD

Use this for your Bruschetta bread!

1 loaf of your favorite sliced Gluten Free Bread

Olive oil

2-3 whole garlic cloves, peeled

1. Cut each slice in half on the diagonal and then quarter each slice diagonally.

2. Spray or brush with olive oil, place on a baking sheet.

3. Toast in the oven (375°) or toaster oven until golden.

4. Rub each piece with the whole garlic cloves while still hot to impart the garlic flavor.

5. Serve with your favorite bruschetta.

ITALIAN GLUTEN FREE CRISPS FOR DIPPING

These are good to dip into flavored olive oil with Italian meals

Gluten Free Pizza Crusts (like Udi's brand)

Olive oil

Grated Parmesan cheese

1. Cut pizza crusts into eighths

2. Spray with olive oil and top with a little fresh grated parmesan cheese

3. Toast under the broiler.

4. Dip into flavored olive oil or pizza sauce.

OLIVE OIL DIP FOR ITALIAN BREAD

"Dip your bread in seasoned olive oil for your next Italian meal."

1/4 cup olive oil

5 cloves garlic

2 tablespoons balsamic vinegar

2 tablespoons Parmesan cheese

1 tablespoon crushed dried oregano

Fresh ground black pepper, to taste

1. Pour the olive oil onto a salad plate. Using a garlic press, press each garlic clove onto the salad plate. Press a garlic clove on one spot and another on another spot to total 5 spots.

2. Drizzle the balsamic vinegar over the oil and garlic. Sprinkle with Parmesan cheese and oregano. Season all this with black pepper and then mix slightly in a "Z" pattern.

3. Dip in your Italian bread or Italian Crisps.

GARLIC BREAD SEASONING

This is one recipe not to miss making....Awesome!

1/2 cup powdered Parmesan cheese

2 tsp. dried basil

2 tsp. salt

2 tsp. dried marjoram

2 Tbs. garlic powder

2 tsp. dried parsley

2 tsp. dried oregano

1. Shake ingredients together in an airtight container.

2. Store this in refrigerator for up to 3 months.

3. *To Make:* Mix 1-1/2 Tbs. of Garlic Bread Seasoning with 1/2 cup soft butter. Spread on French bread and broil or spread on salmon pieces before cooking. You can also sprinkle on vegetables, baked potatoes, fish or chicken.

OH, DO YOU KNOW THE MUFFIN MAN?

There are more muffin recipes in the Quick Breads Section Below to enjoy

6 WEEK BRAN MUFFINS

These muffins cannot be made Gluten Free!

2 cups boiling water

2 cups 100% Bran cereal

2 cups sugar

1 cup oil

4 eggs

5 cups flour

2 tsp. salt

5 tsp. baking soda

1 quart buttermilk

4 cups Bran Flakes or Raisin Bran cereal

1. Pour 2 cups of boiling water over 2 cups 100% Bran and let cool.

2. Beat together 2 cups sugar, 1 cup oil, and 4 eggs in a large bowl.

3. Sift together 5 cups flour, 2 tsp. salt, and 5 tsp. baking soda. Add alternately to the cooled bran with 1 quart buttermilk. Stir in 4 cups of Bran Flakes or Raisin Bran.

4. This mix keeps 4 to 6 weeks in a covered contained in the refrigerator. The mix is best if left overnight in the refrigerator before the first use. (To use just dip off the top of the mix and don't stir.) Place in muffin tins. Bake 15-20 minutes at 375 degrees.

ANNETTE'S PUMPKIN MUFFINS

Makes about 12-16 muffins

1 cup raisins

1/2 cup very hot water

2 eggs

1 cup canned pumpkin

1-1/4 cup sugar

3/4 tsp. cloves

3/4 tsp. cinnamon

1/2 tsp. salt

1/3 cup oil

1-3/4 cup flour (use Featherlight GF mix and 1 tsp. Xanthan)

1-1/2 tsp. baking powder

1/2 tsp. baking soda

1. Soak 1 cup raisins in 1/2 cup very hot water for 5 minutes —don't drain

2. Beat 2 eggs in a bowl and then mix in: pumpkin, sugar, salt, cloves, cinnamon, and 1/3 cup of oil (GF decrease 1 Tbs.)

3. Sift and add in: 1-3/4 cup flour (GF mix & 1 tsp. Xanthan), 1-1/2 tsp. baking powder and 1/2 tsp. baking soda

4. Mix in the raisins and raisin water. Fill muffin tins 2/3 full. Bake at 400 degrees for 25 minutes. Serve.

RHUBARB MUFFINS (GLUTEN FREE)

1-1/4 cups brown sugar

2-1/2 cups gluten free flour mix – your choice

1 tsp. Xanthan

1/2 cup oil

1 tsp. baking soda

1 egg

1 tsp. baking powder

2 tsp. vanilla

1/2 tsp. salt

1 cup buttermilk or sour milk

1/2 cup nuts-optional

1/2 cups diced rhubarb

Topping:

1 or 2 tsp. melted butter

1/3 cup sugar

1 tsp. cinnamon

1. Combine topping ingredients and set aside.

2. Combine wet ingredients & mix with dry ingredients.

3. Put in muffin tins. Sprinkle on topping. Bake 400 F for 15-20 minutes

ONE-BOWL ZUCCHINI BANANA MUFFINS

1/2 cup butter, melted

1/2 cup brown sugar

1/4 cup sugar

1 large egg

2 tsp. vanilla

1-1/2 cups flour (Use a GF flour mix & add 3/4 tsp. Xanthan gum for Gluten Free)

1 tsp. baking soda

1 tsp. cinnamon

1/8 tsp. nutmeg

1 medium banana, mashed (1/2 cup)

1-1/2 cups grated zucchini

Chocolate chips—optional

1. Preheat oven to 350 degrees. Line 12 muffin cups with paper liners.

2. In a large glass bowl, melt butter in microwave. Add sugar, egg, and vanilla; stir.

3. Add flour and spices and stir in. Add banana and zucchini and stir until combined.

4. Fill liners 3/4 full and bake 15-20 minutes.

88

GLUTEN FREE / DAIRY FREE PEANUT BUTTER BANANA CHOCOLATE CHIP MINI BLENDER MUFFINS

The fastest and easiest batter I've ever made. The muffins are gluten-free, grain-free, soy-free, dairy-free, oil-free, refined sugar-free, and they're under 100 calories each (66 calories if you omit chocolate chips). Yield about 17 mini muffins

1 medium ripe banana, peeled

1 large egg

Heaping 1/2 cup creamy regular peanut butter; not natural or homemade peanut butter

3 tablespoons honey (agave or maple syrup may be substituted)

1 tablespoon vanilla extract

1/4 teaspoon baking soda

Pinch salt, optional and to taste

Heaping 1/2 cup mini semi-sweet chocolate chips

1. Preheat oven to 400 degrees F. Prepare mini muffin pans by spraying very well with cooking spray, or grease and flour (GF flour) the pans; set aside. If keeping gluten-free for health reasons, simply use cooking spray or grease the pan.

2. To the canister of a blender, add first 7 ingredients, through optional salt, and blend on high speed until smooth and creamy, about 1 minute.

3. Add chocolate chips and stir in by hand; don't use the blender because it will pulverize them.

4. Using a tablespoon or small cookie scoop that's been sprayed with cooking spray (helps batter slide off spoon or scoop easily), form rounded 1 tablespoon mounds and place mounds into prepared pans. Each cavity should be filled to a solid 3/4 full.

5. Bake for 8 to 9 minutes, or until the tops are set, domed, springy to the touch, and a toothpick inserted into the center comes out clean, or with a few moist crumbs, but no batter. Due to their small size and oven variance, make sure to watch your muffins closely, and bake until done.

6. Allow muffins to cool in pans for about 10 minutes, or until they've firmed up and are cool enough to handle. Muffins are best fresh, but will keep airtight at room temperature for up to 5 days, or in the freezer for up to 4 months.

QUICK BREADS TO ENJOY

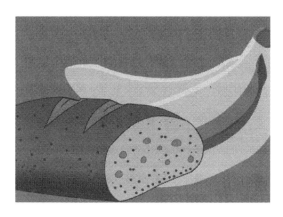

BAKING POWDER BISCUITS

1-3/4 cups flour (use GF flour mix and 3/4 tsp. Xanthan)

1 Tbs. baking powder

1/2 tsp. salt

1/3 cup margarine

3/4 cup milk

1. Preheat oven to 450°F. Mix flour, baking powder and salt in large bowl. Cut in margarine until mixture resembles coarse crumbs. Add milk; stir with fork until soft dough forms.

2. Place dough on lightly floured surface; knead 20 times or until smooth. Pat or roll lightly until dough is 1/2-inch thick. Cut with floured 2-inch cookie cutter to make 16 biscuits, rerolling dough scraps as necessary. Place on ungreased baking sheet.

3. Bake 10 minutes or until golden brown.

GLUTEN FREE BUTTERMILK DROP BISCUITS

2/3 cup rice flour

1/4 cup potato starch

1 Tbs. tapioca starch

2 tsp. baking powder

1/2 tsp. Xanthan

1/4 tsp. salt

1/4 tsp. cream of tartar

1 egg, slightly beaten

1/4 cup oil

1/2 cup buttermilk (or sour milk, just add 1 tsp. lemon juice or vinegar to sour)

1. In a mixing bowl, combine all the dry ingredients.

2. In another bowl, combine the wet ingredients.

3. Stir wet ingredients into dry ingredients and stir until well blended.

4. Drop by large spoonfuls (1/4 cup) onto a greased baking sheet.

5. Bake at 400 degrees for 12 to 15 minutes. Makes 6 to 8 large biscuits

NOTE:
- ✓ _These are also great for strawberry shortcake, breakfast biscuits, biscuits and gravy..._

CHEDDAR DROP BISCUITS

Our favorite!

2 cups flour (GF mix & 1 tsp. Xanthan gum)

2 tsp. baking powder

1/2 tsp. baking soda

1 Tbs. sugar

1/2 tsp. salt

Pinch cayenne pepper

6 Tbs. cold butter cut into small cubes

8 ounces sharp cheese, shredded – 2 cups

1-1/3 cups buttermilk or soured milk with 2 tsp. lemon juice added

3 Tbs. chopped chives

1. In a large bowl whisk together the dry ingredients. Work in butter until it is pea size.

2. Stir in cheddar cheese. Add buttermilk & chives.

3. Mix until dough just comes together. With 2 spoons drop 1/4 cup of dough on 2 parchment-lined baking sheets 2 inches apart.

4. Bake at 425 degrees for 12-14 minutes rotating pans once-- put racks in upper third and lower third of oven.

SUGGESTION
- ✓ *Add garlic salt instead of the salt for garlic biscuits*
- ✓ *Add a combination of chives, thyme, sage etc. for* _herb_ *biscuits (1/2 cup total).*

BARBARA HURST'S CORNBREAD

Makes 8 x 8 pan

1 cup brown sugar

1 heaping Tablespoon shortening

1 egg

1 cup sour milk or Buttermilk - Add 1 tsp. vinegar or lemon juice to milk to sour

1 cup flour (GF mix & 1/2 tsp. Xanthan gum)

1 cup corn meal

1 tsp. baking soda

1. Mix all together in above order.

2. Bake in greased glass pan at 325 degrees for 20-30 minutes or until golden.

CORNBREAD

Serves 6 to 8

> 5 Tbs. unsalted butter, plus more for the pan
>
> 3/4 cup flour (GF mix & 1/3 tsp. Xanthan)
>
> 3/4 cup cornmeal
>
> 1-1/2 tsp. baking powder
>
> 1/2 tsp. baking soda
>
> 1/2 tsp. salt
>
> 1 cup buttermilk (shake before measure)
>
> 2 large eggs

1. Butter an 8 x 8 pan; set aside. Melt 5 Tbs. butter and let it cool.

2. Whisk together flour, cornmeal, baking powder, baking soda and salt. In a large bowl, whisk the buttermilk and eggs. Add the cooled butter and then add the flour mixture; stir until combined.

3. Pour into pan and bake at 425 degrees for 18-23 minutes until toothpick comes out clean. Cool 10 minutes before serving

GLUTEN FREE CORNBREAD

Use this as a side dish with butter or honey-butter. This can also be used as a main dish with Sloppy Joe sauce, or putting taco toppings on top, or use it in stuffing recipes.

> 1 cup corn meal
>
> 1 cup milk
>
> 1 cup Featherlight flour mix
>
> 1/4 cup oil
>
> 1/2 tsp. xanthan gum
>
> 1 egg
>
> 2-4 Tbs. sugar
>
> 1 Tbs. baking powder

1. Preheat oven to 425 degrees. Combine all dry ingredients in a bowl.

2. In another bowl combine wet ingredients. Combine dry with wet and beat on high speed for 1 minute. Pour into a well-greased 8x8 or 9x13 pan.

3. Bake 12 to 15 minutes for 8x8 pan and 20 to 25 minutes for a 9x13 pan.

SPOONBREAD

Nicholeen Peck's

4 Tbs. butter

Brown sugar

4 cups milk

12 Tbs. butter (3/4 cup)

2 cups cornmeal

1 tsp. salt

6 eggs

1. Preheat oven to 350 degrees. Place 4 Tbs. butter into 9x13 baking dish in the oven until the butter melts; remove pan from oven. Sprinkle a generous amount of brown sugar on the bottom of the pan.

2. In a sauce pan, on the stove, scald 4 cups milk; stir in 12 Tbs. butter (3/4 cup), 2 cups cornmeal, and 1 tsp. salt.

3. Cook, stirring constantly, until cornmeal comes away from sides of the pan and mixture thickens. Set aside to cool until lukewarm.

4. Separate 6 eggs at room temperature. Beat the egg yolks and mix them into cornmeal mixture in the sauce pan. Beat the egg whites until stiff peaks form and fold them in; mix gently but well.

5. Pour mixture into your prepared 9x13 baking dish. Bake for 1 hour or until golden brown. Serve Immediately.

CORN TORTILLAS

1 cup Masa Harina (Corn Flour)
1/4 cup white rice flour
1/2 cup Xanthan Gum
1/2 tsp. salt
1 cup hot, but not boiling water

1. Place corn flour, rice flour, xanthan gum, and salt in a bowl. Add the water and mix with your hands to make dough that comes together in a soft ball.

2. Place on corn floured board and knead until the dough is elastic enough to not crack.

3. Divide into 15 equal portions and cover with damp towel. Roll and or press into 6 inch circles between wax paper or plastic wrap and smooth edges. Set aside. Finish the rest of the dough.

4. Cook on a hot griddle or hot frying pan and cook for 30 seconds, turn over and cook another 30-60 seconds, turning once more and let the tortilla puff slightly but yet it is still soft and pliable (about 15-30 seconds).

5. Remove to towel and fold over the other part of towel over it. Cook the next one and continue until the dough is used up. Serve immediately. These may be stored in refrigerator for up to a week. Best if used fresh.

BRAZILIAN CHEESE BUNS (PAO DE QUEIJO)

1-1/2 cups tapioca starch
1/4 cup cream
1/4 cup water
1 Tbs. butter
1/2 tsp. salt
1 egg, beaten
1/2 grated hard cheese; sharp, parmesan, etc.

1. In a saucepan, combine the cream, water, butter, and salt and bring to a simmer on medium-low heat. You want to get it to the point that it's starting to bubble, but not boiling. In a large bowl, add the tapioca starch. Add the starch to the cream mixture (it will clump), and stir it together. Let it cool for 5 minutes.

2. As it is cooling, preheat oven to 400 degrees.

3. Add the egg and knead it in with your hands—messy! Add the cheese and knead. Roll the dough into 1" balls (15-20). Put them on a baking sheet and bake 15-20 minutes, until golden brown.

4. These keep for a few days in a container and microwaved to warm. You can freeze them prior to baking so that you can have them ready 20-25 minutes after taking out of the freezer. (Spices can also be added for flavor.)

BRAZILIAN CHEESE BREAD

For Gluten Free rolls, pizza, and crackers

> **2 cups tapioca starch**
>
> **1 Tbs. baking powder**
>
> **1/4 tsp. salt**
>
> **1 cup finely grated cheese (I use Pecorino Romano for rolls and pizza and 1/2 to 1 cup sharp cheese for crackers)**
>
> **3 large eggs**
>
> **1 Tbs. olive oil**
>
> **3 Tbs. milk**

1. Mix dry ingredients and then add wet ingredients. Mix until consistency of cookie dough. You might need to add more tapioca starch or milk--about 2 Tbs.--until it is right. It can be refrigerated for 1 hour now.

2. Rolls: It needs to be on the moist side. Spray non-stick spray on your hands and shape into about 12 balls. Bake 375 for 12-15 minutes. For pizza crust, pat out on a pizza pan, add toppings and bake as above. For crackers, roll thin, cut into squares, bake until light brown and crisp.

GLUTEN FREE SCONES

These are great with any soup, stew, salad or as Navajo tacos or just with butter and honey!

4 cups Featherlight mix

1 Tbs. yeast

1 Tbs. xanthan gum

1 egg

2 tsp. unflavored gelatin

1/3 egg whites

2 tsp. egg replacer

1 tsp. salt

1/4 cup sugar

1/3 c. butter (cut into chunks)

1/2 cup dry milk powder

3 Tbs. honey

2 cups water

4 cups vegetable oil

1 tsp. rice vinegar

1. Combine dry ingredients in a bowl.

2. In a bowl of a stand mixer whisk the egg, egg whites, butter, rice vinegar and honey. Add water. With mixer on low, slowly add dry ingredients to the egg mixture. Beat the mixture on high for 3-1/2 minutes.

3. Beat in an additional 1/4 cup of Featherlight mix. Dough will be quite sticky. Covering your hands with Featherlight mix, take out about 1/4 cup of the dough and pat it flat—approximately 1/4-inch thick.

4. Heat oil to 350 degrees in deep skillet or fryer. Fry dough until brown, approximately 2-4 minutes each side, turning once.

JANEEN'S BANANA BREAD

This Makes 2-3 Loaves

1 cube soft butter (1/2 cup)

2 cups sugar

4 eggs

1 tsp. vanilla

4 cups flour (use GF mix & 2 tsp. Xanthan)

5 bananas mashed

2 tsp. baking soda

1/2 cup chopped nuts – optional

1. Cream butter and sugar; mix in eggs and vanilla.

2. Add flour and baking soda and mix. Add the bananas. Mix well and add nuts.

3. Pour into greased small to medium size loaf pans. Bake 325 degrees for 25 to 50 minutes plus. Bake until toothpick comes out clean. Remove from pans, turn on side, and cool on a rack. Baking time varies depending on pan size.

GLUTEN FREE BANANA BREAD

5 Tbsp. unsalted butter – room temp.

1 cup sugar

2 eggs

1-1/2 cups mashed bananas (about 4 small)

1 cup brown rice flour

3/4 cup millet flour

1 tsp. baking soda

1/2 tsp. salt

1/2 tsp. xanthan gum

1/4 tsp. baking powder

1/2 chopped walnuts (optional)

1. Preheat oven to 350 degrees. Line a 9 x 5 inch loaf pan with foil and spray with cooking spray.

2. Beat butter and sugar until light yellow and fluffy with mixer on high. Add eggs & mix in. Add banana and 1/3 cup water and mix for 1 minute. Sprinkle dry ingredients over the batter and nuts and then mix just until combined.

3. Pour into greased loaf pans. Bake 50-55 minutes until loaf springs back to touch.

4. Cool 5 minutes, lift out of pan and cool completely. (10 slices, 260 calories, 2 g. fiber)

THE BEST GLUTEN FREE BANANA BREAD

My Favorite GF Banana Bread!

This recipe works well with small loaf pans or muffin tins. It is dense, moist, flavorful, and never crumbly. The addition of blueberries, cranberries or chocolate chips is a great addition!

1⁄2 cup butter or non-dairy alternative

3⁄4 cup sugar

2 eggs (or egg substitute)

1 tsp. gluten free vanilla

1⁄2 cup sour cream (dairy or non-dairy)

1 cup mashed, ripe banana (approx. 2 bananas)

1-1⁄2 cups Jules GF flour mix with Xanthan (or Featherlight mix with 1 tsp. xanthan gum)

2 Tbs. flaxseed meal (optional)--I always add this!

1 tsp. baking soda

2 tsp. gluten-free baking powder

Dash of salt

Chocolate chips, optional

Blueberries or other berries of choice, optional

1. Preheat oven to 350 degrees. Oil 1 loaf pan or 4 small loaf pans or approximately 16 muffin cups.

2. Cream butter and sugar until mixture is light and fluffy. Add eggs and vanilla and beat well. Mix in sour cream and bananas until well blended.

3. In a separate bowl, whisk the dry ingredients and then add gradually into wet mixture until mixed. Lastly, gently stir in berries or chocolate chips if using.

4. Spoon batter into prepared pans. Bake approximately 1 hour for 1 loaf; 35-45 minutes for smaller pans; or approximately 30 minutes for muffins. Test with a cake tester until clean. Cool.

ANNETTE'S BANANA BREAD OR MUFFINS

This can be gluten and dairy free!

1/2 cup shortening

1/2 cup brown sugar

1/2 cup white sugar

3 tsp. milk or almond milk

2 eggs

1 cup mashed banana (about 3)

1 cup flour (GF use Featherlight mix or 3/4 c. rice flour, 3 Tbs. potato starch, 1 Tbs. tapioca starch, and 1/2 tsp. Xanthan

1 tsp. baking soda

½ tsp. baking powder

1 tsp. vanilla

1 tsp. pure Maple syrup

Toasted walnuts or pecans to add on top - optional

1. Cream together: 1/2 cup shortening, 1/2 cup brown sugar, 1/2 cup white sugar

2. Add: 3 tsp. milk and 2 eggs. Mix in 1 cup mashed banana (3), 1 cup flour (use Favorite GF mix and 1/2 tsp. Xanthan), and 1 tsp. baking soda

3. Add: 1 tsp. vanilla, and also 1 tsp. pure Maple syrup. Pour into large 9 x 5 greased loaf pan.

4. Bake at 325 degrees for 1 hour 20 min plus or minus (Bake muffins 15-20 min.)

5. Optional: Add toasted walnuts/pecans (toast 5-10 min. at 350 degrees) on top before baking.

PUMPKIN BREAD

Makes 2 loaves (9 x 5 x 3)

3 cups sugar

1 cup oil

2/3 cup water

4 eggs

2 cups canned pumpkin (1 small can)

3-1/2 cups flour (GF use mix and 1-3/4 tsp. Xanthan)

1-1/2 tsp. salt

2 tsp. baking soda

1 tsp. cinnamon

2 cups raisins or chocolate chips

1 cup chopped walnuts - optional

1. Dissolve and mix 3 cups sugar in 1 cup oil and 2/3 cup water. Mix in 4 eggs and 2 cups pumpkin (1 can).

2. Add 3-1/2 cups flour (GF mix & 1-3/4 tsp. Xanthan gum) , 1-1/2 tsp. salt, 2 tsp. baking soda, 1 tsp. cinnamon, 1/2 tsp. nutmeg and mix well.

3. Add 2 cups raisins or chocolate chips and 1 cup chopped walnuts (optional).

4. Pour into 2 greased loaf pans. Bake at 350 degrees for 1 hour. Remove and cool.

MOTHER'S RICH ZUCCHINI BREAD OR CAKE

3 eggs

1 cup oil

2-1/2 cups sugar

3 tsp. vanilla

1 tsp. baking soda

1/4 tsp. baking powder

1 tsp. salt

2 tsp. cinnamon

1/2 tsp. nutmeg - optional

2 to 3 cups grated zucchini

3 cups flour (use GF mix plus 1-1/2 tsp. Xanthan)

1/2 to 1 cup chopped nuts - optional

1. Mix together 3 eggs, 1 cup oil, 2-1/2 cups sugar, and 2 tsp. vanilla

2. Stir in 1 tsp. baking soda, 1/2 tsp. baking powder, 1 tsp. salt, and 2 tsp. cinnamon & optional 1/2 tsp. nutmeg

3. Add 2-3 cups grated zucchini (remove seeds), 3 cups flour (GF mix plus 1-1/2 tsp. Xanthan gum) and optional 1/2 to 1 cup nuts

4. Bake in 2 loaf pans or a Bundt pan at 325 degrees for 60-70 minutes. Cool & drizzle with lemon icing, optional.

5. *Lemon Icing:* Blend together: 1 tsp. melted butter, 1 tsp. milk, 1 tsp. lemon juice and 1 cup powdered sugar and drizzle on cooled cakes.

ZUCCHINI BREAD OR MUFFINS

Nicholeen Peck's   *Gluten free is in parentheses.*

1 cup sugar

1 cup brown sugar

3 large eggs, beaten

1 cup oil

2-3 cups grated zucchini

3 tsp. vanilla

3 cups flour (Mix 1-1/2 cups GF flour mix & 1-1/2 cups Featherlight flour mix plus 2 tsp. xanthan gum for Gluten Free)

1 tsp. soda

1 tsp. salt

1 Tbs. cinnamon

1 tsp. allspice

1 tsp. nutmeg

1 tsp. cloves

1/2 tsp. baking powder

2/3 cup chocolate chips

1. Mix all ingredients and either place in greased loaf pan or muffin tins.

2. Bake loaves for 1 hour at 325 degrees and muffins for 18-22 minutes at 350 degrees.

BEVERAGES TO SIP

Smoothie recipes are found in the "Breakfast Anyone?" section

106

BRAZILIAN LIME-ADE

This is similar to the one at Rodizio Grill

3 Limes

2-3 Tbsp. Sweetened Condensed Milk

1/2 cup sugar

3 cup water

1. Wash limes and cut off ends. Slice into wedges.

2. Place all ingredients in blender; blend until creamy. Don't blend too long or it will be bitter.

3. Strain and serve over ice.

LIMEADE

5 to 7 limes, plus more slices for garnish

1/2 cup sugar or honey; plus more is needed

5 cups water, divided

1. Roll limes back & forth on counter with palm of hand. Cut limes in half, and juice them by hand, with a juicer or a reamer. Reserve the rinds. (You should have 1/2 cup juice.) Transfer juice and rinds to a large pitcher.

2. Bring 1 cup water to a boil in a small saucepan. Add the sugar or honey, and stir until dissolved. Pour syrup into pitcher and add 4 cups water. Stir until blended. Refrigerate 1 hour. Discard lime rinds.

3. Serve garnished with lime slices.

PINEAPPLE PLANTER'S PUNCH

4 cups unsweetened pineapple juice

2 cups orange juice – fresh or frozen

1/2 cup fresh lemon juice

2 liters ginger-ale, chilled

1. Mix first 3 ingredients and chill 2 or more hours.

2. Stir in ginger ale and serve over ice.

RHUBARB SPARKLER AND CITRUS-COOKED RHUBARB SYRUP

Citrus-Cooked Rhubarb Syrup

1 lb. rhubarb--3-1/4 cups

1/2 cup orange juice

1/2 cup honey

1/4 cup water

2 tsp. finely grated orange zest

Seltzer or Sprite

1. Simmer 1 lb. coarsely chopped rhubarb (3-1/4 cups) with 1/2 cup each orange juice and honey, 1/4 cup water, and 2 tsp finely grated orange zest until rhubarb is tender, 1 minute.

2. Strain rhubarb through sieve set over bowl to catch juices. Cool liquid and solids in separate bowls. (Makes 1-3/4 cups rhubarb and 1 -1/4 cups syrup.)

3. Chill in airtight container. This syrup can also be poured over ice cream etc.

RHUBARB SPARKLER:

1/4 cup citrus-cooked rhubarb syrup

Ice

Seltzer or Sprite

1. Pour 1/4 cup of reserved citrus-cooked rhubarb syrup into a glass filled with ice

2. Top it off with either seltzer or Sprite.

WENDY'S STYLE FROSTY

3/4 cup milk

4 cups vanilla ice cream

1/4 cup Nestle' Quick Chocolate powder

1. Combine in blender until smooth.

2. Serves 2

FROZEN HOT CHOCOLATE

3 oz. of your favorite chocolates (kisses, chocolate chips, Hershey bars etc.)

2 tsp. store bought hot chocolate mix

1-1/2 Tbs. sugar

1-1/2 cups milk

3 cups ice

Whipped cream for garnish

Chocolate shavings for garnish

1. Chop chocolate into small pieces and place in top of double boiler over simmering water and stir until melted. Add cocoa and sugar; stirring until blended.

2. Remove from heat and slowly add 1/2 cup of milk and stir. Cool to room temperature.

3. In a blender place 1 cup milk, the room temperature chocolate, and ice. Blend on high until smooth. Pour into giant goblet and garnish with cream and chocolate shavings.

4. Serves 1 or 2

ORANGE JULIUS

1 (6-ounce) can of frozen orange juice concentrate

1 cup water

1 cup milk

2 Tbsp. nonfat dry milk (optional)

1/2 tsp. vanilla

1/4 tsp. sugar

6 to 18 ice cubes

1. Combine all ingredients except ice in blender. Blend at high speed, adding ice cubes until mixture is thick & slushy.

2. Serve immediately.

HOT ORANGE DRINK--WASSAIL MIX

2 cups powdered orange drink mix

1-1/3 cups sugar

1/2 tsp. ground cloves

3 Tbs. powdered lemonade mix

1 tsp. cinnamon

1. Mix all ingredients. Put in a 1 quart air tight container and store in cupboard.

2. To serve: Add 2-3 tsp. to 1 cup hot water.

3. To make a breakfast drink: Add 6 Tbs. per qt. of water

HOT WASSAIL

Use a slow cooker to keep it warm for entertaining.

1 (12-ounce) can of frozen orange juice concentrate

1 (6-ounce) can of frozen lemonade concentrate

2 quarts water

1 gallon apple cider or juice

5 cinnamon sticks

5 whole cloves

1. Combine all ingredients in a pan. Simmer 10 minutes. Remove spices. Keep hot.

2. Delicious cold, too.

LEMON CREAM SODA

1 cup lemon curd—(recipe on p.228)—or use a store-bought one

One 1-liter sparkling water, chilled

8 scoops vanilla ice cream—or about 1-1/2 pint

1. Spoon 1/4 cup lemon curd into each of 4 pint glasses.

2. Add 1/4 cup sparkling water and stir to combine.

3. Add 2 scoops of ice cream to each glass and fill with more sparkling water. Enjoy!

FRUIT FIZZ

Good replacement for soft drinks

1 cup unsweetened fruit juice; any flavor

1 cup sparkling water (no-salt variety)

1. Mix fruit juice and sparkling water adding more or less of either to taste.

2. Serve over ice.

MADELINE'S LEMONADE

6 large lemons, juiced (1-1/2 cups juice).

2 limes, juiced (1/3 cup)

1 cup sugar

6 cups of water

1 cup fresh raspberries/strawberries

1. In a 2 quart pitcher combine juice from 6 large lemons (1-1/2 cups juice). Add juice of 2 limes (1/3 cup), 1 cup sugar, and 6 cups of water.

2. Add 1 cup fresh raspberries/strawberries; cover and chill overnight in refrigerator.

3. Serve over ice. Garnish with lemon slices. Serves 8

STRAWBERRY LEMONADE

Make 7 cups

1 cup frozen sweetened strawberries, thawed

6 cups cold water

1/2 cup sugar

1 cup fresh lemon juice (from 6-9 lemons)

1. Blend strawberries, 1 cup water, and sugar about 1 minute.

2. Strain seeds.

3. Combine with lemon juice and 5 cups water.

4. Serve over ice.

QUICK BANANA SHAKE OR MALT

1 frozen ripe banana (To freeze: peel and slice one banana; place it in a bag & freeze)

3/4 cup milk

1/4 tsp. vanilla

1 Tbs. sugar--optional

3 Tbs. malt powder (optional) - leave out for just a shake

1. Blend all in a blender until smooth.

2. If you do have not a frozen banana, use a regular one and 7 ice cubes.

3. This is a low calorie ice cream like treat...

BANANA-STRAWBERRY FRUIT SHAKE

1-2 frozen banana pieces—(see Tip below)

2-3 frozen strawberries

1-1/2 cups orange juice

2-3 Tbs. plain or vanilla yogurt (optional)

1. Place all ingredients in a blender.

2. Cover and blend until all fruit is totally blended and mixture is thick and slushy. Serve.

3. *Tip:* For frozen banana pieces; cut ripe bananas into 8-10 pieces each and freeze flat in a ziploc bag. For Strawberries; cut each in half or pieces and freeze in a ziploc bag.

NOTE:
   ✓ *When strawberries are out of season, use any kind of juice: cranberry, peach, tropical, etc. May use less orange juice and more bananas if desired.*

PEACH SLUSH

This was our snack before bed with toast. My dad made these all the time.

1 quart bottled peaches or 1 (29-oz.) can

3-4 ice cubes

1. Pour peaches in blender. Add ice cubes until blender is 3/4 full.

2. Cover and blend until mix is slushy. This works for any bottled fruit. YUM!

RASPBERRY PUNCH

1 2-liter bottle of Sprite, chilled

1/2 gallon raspberry sherbet

1. In a large punch bowl, pour in 1 2-liter bottle of Sprite.

2. Place 1/2 gallon of raspberry sherbet (or any flavor), in by teaspoons. Do not stir. Serve.

FRUIT JUICE COOLER

1 cup fruit juice; any flavor

1 cup Sprite or Club Soda

1. Mix fruit juice and add Sprite.

2. Serve over ice cubes.

HOMEMADE DRY ICE ROOT BEER

Serves 90-100

4 pounds sugar

5 pounds dry ice

5 gallons water

1 bottle root beer extract

1. In a 5 gallon container, mix sugar, water and extract well.

2. Add dry ice. Let stand 30 minutes before serving.

BANANA SLUSHY PUNCH

Serves 25

4 cups sugar

6 cups water

2-1/2 cups orange juice

1/2 cup lemon juice

5 bananas, mashed

4 cups pineapple juice

Ginger-ale or lemon-lime soda pop

1. Heat water and sugar until dissolved. Add juices and bananas. Freeze.

2. Scrape slush into glasses and pour ginger-ale or lemon-lime soda on top.

3. Can also break the frozen mixture into chunks to put in a punch bowl with soda pop.

BANANA PINEAPPLE SUMMER FREEZE

2 cups cold water

6 large bananas

1 (46-oz.) can pineapple juice

1 (12-oz.) can of frozen orange juice concentrate

1 (20-oz.) can crushed pineapple

1 (6-oz.) can of frozen lemonade concentrate

Sprite soda pop

1. In a blender, place 2 cups water and the bananas; blend until smooth.

2. Put in a 1 gallon container or a 9 x 13 container. Mix in the rest of the ingredients.

3. Cover and freeze. For easier scooping, take out of the freezer 30 minutes before serving.

4. Fill each glass half full of slush and pour Sprite over the top.

FRUIT SLUSH

Bernice Gundry's

> **3-1/2 cups water**
>
> **2 cups sugar**
>
> **1 can (20 oz.) crushed pineapple**
>
> **1 can (6 oz.) of frozen orange juice concentrate**
>
> **1 pkg. frozen raspberries or strawberries, crushed**
>
> **Sprite soda pop**

1. Boil the sugar and water and let cool.

2. Add crushed pineapple, frozen orange juice concentrate, and 1 pkg. raspberries, crushed. Freeze in a plastic container. Stir every hour for the first 2 to 3 hours.

3. About 1 hour before serving, take out to soften.

4. Spoon some into cups and add a small amount of Sprite right before serving. Serves 15-20

FROZEN FRUIT SLUSH

> **6 oranges-juiced or (1-12-ounce can of frozen orange juice concentrate)**
>
> **6 lemons-juiced or (1-12-ounce can of frozen lemonade concentrate)**
>
> **6 limes-juice or (1-12-ounce can of frozen limeade concentrate)**
>
> **6 bananas-smashed**
>
> **1 cup water**
>
> **Sprite soda pop**

1. Mix all together and freeze in a container.

2. Stir twice while it's freezing.

3. Take out of freezer 30 minutes before serving. Scoop some into cups and pour on Sprite.

JANEEN'S HOT CHRISTMAS EVE PUNCH

2 cups sugar

2 cups water

1 (6 oz.) can of frozen orange juice concentrate

3/4 cup lemon juice or 1 (6 oz.) can of lemonade concentrate

2 quarts water

2 tsp. vanilla

1 tsp. almond extract

Red food coloring

1. Boil 2 cups sugar and 2 cups water; then add one (6-ounce can) frozen orange juice concentrate and also 1 (6-ounce) can of water.

2. Mix and add 3/4 cup lemon juice or 1(6-ounce) can of lemonade.

3. Add 2 quarts water, 2 tsp. vanilla and 1 tsp. almond extract plus some red food coloring.

4. Heat until warm and serve!

HOT CHOCOLATE MIX

1 8-quart box of powdered milk (13 cups)

1 1-lb box of instant chocolate mix (4 cups)

1 (6-ounce) bottle non-dairy creamer or 1-1/2 cup plus 2 Tbs.

1 1-lb. bag powdered sugar (4-3/4 cups)

1. Mix all together and store in a tightly covered container.

2. To make 1 cup: To 3/4 cup hot water add 1/4 cup mix and stir. Enjoy or add marshmallows!

LIME PUNCH

Tara Schippanboord

1 pkg. 6-ounce lime gelatin

2 cups boiling water

1 (12-ounce) can of frozen limeade

1 cup lime juice

1 tsp. almond extract

3 liter of Sprite or 7-up

1. Dissolve the gelatin in boiling water. Mix in the rest of the ingredients except Sprite.

2. Pour into a punch bowl and add 3 liters of Sprite or 7-up.

3. If you would like to have a frozen ring of ice….freeze cherry 7-up in the ring with red food coloring. Float the ring on top of the punch in the bowl.

MINT SIMPLE SYRUP

1/2 cup fresh mint leaves, packed

2 cups sugar

2 cups water

1. Stir in 1/2 cup fresh mint with 2 cups sugar and 2 cups water. Bring to just boiling. Stir until the sugar is dissolved.

2. Let stand 2 hours before straining. The flavor becomes stronger the longer it steeps. Strain out leaves and chill.

3. Use in lemonade mixes or add some to club soda etc.

FRESH MINT HERBAL TEA

When mint is exploding in the garden, make this or use it to soothe upset stomachs

12 large sprigs of fresh mint

4 cups boiling water, or more

4 tsp. honey (optional-I have never used it)

1. Wash mint and place into a pitcher. Pour boiling water over and steep 4 minutes.

2. Strain and serve with a teaspoon of honey in each cup…This can also be chilled with the honey added to the pitcher.

3. I love this one hot in the winter or chilled in the summer! Enjoy one of my Favorites!

FRESH MINT PUNCH

2-1/2 cups water

2 cups sugar

2 cups fresh mint leaves and stalks

6 lemons, juiced and the grated zest

2 oranges, juice and the grated zest

1. In a saucepan, combine water and sugar and bring to a boil. Boil over low heat for 10 minutes.

2. Put mint, lemon juice, oranges juice and zests in a large bowl. Pour boiling syrup over. Cover tightly and let cool.

3. Strain syrup through several thicknesses of cheesecloth and store in the refrigerator.

4. To serve: Add 5-6 Tbs. of syrup over ice in a glass. Fill glass with water or ginger-ale.

118

APPLE OR GRAPE SODA

2 cups chilled unsweetened apple or grape juice

2 tsp. lemon or lime juice

2 cups chilled club soda (or Sprite)

1. Combine all the juices.

2. Add club soda very slowly and gently stir.

3. Serve over ice.

NICHOLEEN'S MOCK DOLE WHIP

Nicholeen's favorite Hawaiian treat!

2 cups cold pineapple juice

3/4 cup sugar

1 cup heavy cream

1/2 tsp. vanilla

Pinch of salt

1. Whisk the juice and sugar until the sugar dissolves.

2. Stir in cream, vanilla and salt.

3. Unless the juice was very cold to begin with, chill the mixture in the refrigerator for a couple of hours or over an ice bath for 20 to 30 minutes.

4. Freeze in an ice cream freezer. Let it harden in freezer for a few hours. Scoop and enjoy!

MOCK SANGRIA

2 cups orange juice

1 cup white grape juice

1 cup cranberry juice

1 liter lemon-lime soda

Ice cubes

Fresh mint sprigs to garnish with

2 cups assorted fresh fruit (oranges, cut into wedges; sliced lemons or limes; pineapple wedges; seedless red or green grapes; sliced peaches; and halved strawberries)

1. In a large bowl or pitcher, stir together all juices. Add lemon-lime soda; stir gently.

2. Fill 10 glasses with ice. Divide fruit among glasses.

3. Pour juice mix over and garnish with mint.

ITALIAN SODAS

Our family loves to have these at all our family dinners. I have many flavors of Torani syrups and we just mix and match all sorts of flavors for unique Italian sodas.

3 Tbs. Italian soda syrup

Crushed ice

Club soda

1 Tbs. half and half

Aerosol whipped cream-optional

1. Measure 3 Tbs. (6 pumps) of syrup into the bottom of a 24-oz cup.

2. Fill the cup halfway with crushed ice.

3. Add club soda to about 1-1/2 inches from top.

4. Add a splash of half and half (1 Tbs.).

5. Stir with a straw and serve.

6. We like aerosol cream on top, too!

PINEAPPLE ICE—1 QUART

1 cup water

1/2 cup sugar

1 cup crushed pineapple

1/4 cup lemon juice

Sprite

1. Heat 1 cup water and 1/2 cup sugar until dissolved. Remove from heat and chill.

2. Add crushed pineapple and 1/4 cup lemon juice; stir, and freeze. Great added to Sprite.

CAKES AND FROSTINGS

CAKES FOR ALL OCCASIONS

CRAZY CAKE

Mary (Grandma) Gundry - She made this for our Birthdays every year!

2 cups sugar

3 cups flour (use GF mix and 1-1/2 tsp Xanthan)

2 tsp. soda

1/3 cup cocoa

3/4 cup oil

2 tsp. vinegar

1 tsp. vanilla

2 cups warm water

1. Sift together in a large bowl: 2 cups sugar, 3 cups flour (use GF mix and 1-1/2 tsp. Xanthan), 2 tsp. baking soda, and 1/3 cup cocoa.

2. Make 3 wells in the dry ingredients and put in the following: 3/4 cup oil in the 1st well or hole, 2 tsp. vinegar in the 2nd well, and 1 tsp. vanilla in the 3rd well.

3. Pour 2 cups warm water over the top of this mix and BLEND gently together (not beat) with a spoon.

4. Pour into UNGREASED 9x13 pan and bake at 350 for 35-45 minutes.

CHOCOLATE CHIP ZUCCHINI CAKE

(Gluten Free is in parenthesis)

1/2 cup butter

1/2 cup oil

1-3/4 cups sugar

2 eggs

1 tsp. vanilla

1/2 cup sour milk – add 1-1/2 tsp. vinegar to sour the milk

4 Tbs. cocoa (1/4 cup)

1/2 tsp. salt

2-1/2 cups flour (1-3/4 c. rice flour, 1/2 c. potato starch, 1/4 c. tapioca starch, & 1-1/2 tsp. xanthan or use 2-1/2 cups GF flour mix and 1-1/2 tsp. Xanthan)

1/2 tsp. cinnamon

1/2 tsp. cloves

1 tsp. soda

2-3 cups grated zucchini

1 cup chocolate chips

Chopped nuts, optional

1. Cream the butter, oil, and sugar until light and fluffy. Add the eggs and vanilla; mix well. Add the milk and cocoa; blend together.

2. To the creamed mixture above add, 2-1/2 cups flour (1-3/4 c. rice flour, 1/2 c. potato starch, 1/4 c. tapioca starch, & 1-1/2 tsp. xanthan), 1/2 tsp. cinnamon, 1/2 tsp. cloves, 1 tsp. baking powder, and 1 tsp. soda. Blend all together.

3. Blend in 2-3 cups grated zucchini. Pour into a greased & floured 9x13 baking dish.

4. Sprinkle with 1 cup chocolate chips (and chopped nuts if desired).

5. Bake at 350 degrees for 40-50 minutes until toothpick comes out clean.

MOIST APPLESAUCE CAKE

Evah Huish

1/2 cup shortening

1 tsp. cinnamon

2 cups sugar

2 tsp. soda, dissolved in 1/2 cup boiling water

1 egg

1 tsp. vanilla

1-1/2 cup applesauce, not drained

1/2 cup chopped nuts

2-1/2 cups flour (GF mix & 1-1/4 tsp. Xanthan)

1 cup raisins

1/2 tsp. salt

1/2 tsp. cloves

1/2 tsp. allspice

Powdered sugar for icing

Chopped nuts to sprinkle on the top

1. Cream shortening and sugar together. Add applesauce and dry ingredients. Add vanilla, nuts, and raisins.

2. Bake in a 9x13 baking dish at 350 degrees for 45 minutes to an hour.

3. Use a powdered sugar, butter and milk icing- see Buttercream Frosting, p. 158. Sprinkle the top with chopped nuts, if desired.

PUMPKIN PIE SQUARES

Marie Hofmann

1 yellow 2-layer cake mix (use a GF one)

1/2 cup butter, melted

2 eggs

1-1/2 cups pumpkin

3/4 cup sugar

1 large can (11.5 oz.) of evaporated canned milk

1/2 tsp. ginger

1/2 tsp. cloves

1 tsp. cinnamon

3 Tbs. butter

1. From 1 yellow cake mix (use a GF one), remove 1 cup of mix and reserve for top.

2. Mix 1/2 cup butter, melted, with the remaining cake mix powder. Press this into a 9x13 pan.

3. Mix and pour over the crust: 2 eggs, 1-1/2 cups pumpkin, 3/4 cup sugar, 1 lg. can of canned milk, 1/2 tsp. ginger, 1/2 tsp. cloves, and 1 tsp. cinnamon

4. Mix and cut in 3 Tbs. butter into reserved cake mix and sprinkle on top.

5. Bake at 350 degrees for 60 minutes.

HURRY-UP SPICE CAKE

This is one I made all the time as a teenager--loved the crumb topping!

3/4 cup chopped nuts

1/2 cup brown sugar

2 Tbs. flour (use GF)

1 tsp. cinnamon

2 Tbs. butter

1/2 cup shortening

1/2 cup sugar

3/4 cup brown sugar

3 eggs

3 cups flour (use GF and 1-1/2 tsp. Xanthan)

3 tsp. baking powder

1 tsp. salt

1 tsp. cinnamon

1/2 tsp. allspice

1/2 tsp. nutmeg

1 cup milk

1 tsp. vanilla

White icing to drizzle on when hot:

1-1/2 cups powdered sugar

2 - 3 Tbs. milk

1. Make the nut topping by combining: 3/4 cup chopped nuts, 1/2 cup brown sugar, 2 Tbs. flour (GF), 1 tsp. cinnamon, and 2 tbs. butter. Mix well; set aside.

2. Combine: 1/2 cup shortening, 1 cup sugar, and 3/4 cup brown sugar and cream well

3. Add: 3 eggs, one at a time, and beat 1 minute after each one.

4. Whisk together: 3 cups flour (use GF mix & 1-1/2 tsp. Xanthan), 3 tsp. baking powder, 1 tsp. salt, 1 tsp. cinnamon, 1/2 tsp. allspice, and 1/2 tsp. nutmeg

5. Combine: 1 cup milk and 1 tsp. vanilla. Add alternately with dry ingredients; mix in.

6. Spread: Place half of the batter in a well-greased and lightly floured 9x13 pan.

7. Sprinkle with nut-sugar mixture, reserving 1/4 cup for top.

8. Top with remaining batter and 1/4 cup nut mix.

9. Bake: 350 degrees for 50-60 minutes—Drizzle with the thin icing while hot. Enjoy!

THANKSGIVING OR CHRISTMAS PUDDING

Tara Schipaanboord   Love this one!

1 cup sugar

1/2 cup butter

2 eggs

1 cup grated carrots

1 cup chopped nuts

1 cup chopped dates

3/4 cup raisins

1 cup flour (use GF mix and 1/2 tsp. Xanthan)

1 tsp. soda

1 tsp. nutmeg

1 tsp. cinnamon

1/2 tsp. cloves

1-1/2 cups soft bread crumbs (use GF)

1. Cream: 1 cup sugar, 1/2 cup butter and then add 2 eggs; mix well.

2. Stir in: 1 cup grated carrots, 1 cup chopped nuts, 1 cup chopped dates, & 3/4 cup raisins

3. Mix and add: 1 cup flour (GF mix & 1/2 tsp. Xanthan), 1 tsp. soda, 1 tsp. nutmeg, 1 tsp. cinnamon, and 1/2 tsp. cloves

4. Add in: 1-1/2 cup soft bread crumbs (GF)

5. Pour into 2 greased large pumpkin cans or a steamed pudding mold—this is why it is great to make pumpkin pies and this or else save your cans.

6. Steam; covered with tin foil in a pan of water for 2 hours until done. Remove, cool and store in refrigerator, if not eating right then. Serve with either Butter Sauce or Lemon Sauce, p.128.

BUTTER SAUCE

1-1/2 cups sugar

1/2 cup butter

2 cups water

Dash of salt

1-2 Tbs. cornstarch

3 Tbs. water

1. Brown 1-1/2 cups sugar and 1/2 cup butter —then add 2 cups water and a dash of salt.

2. Boil together and thicken with 1-2 Tbs. of cornstarch dissolved in 3 Tbs. cold water.

3. Serve sauce over the top of the Thanksgiving or the Christmas Pudding.

LEMON SAUCE

1 Tbs. cornstarch

1/2 cup sugar

1 cup boiling water

3 Tbs. butter

1 tsp. lemon zest

3 Tbs. lemon juice

1. Mix cornstarch and sugar in a small saucepan. Stir in boiling water.

2. Cook over medium heat, stirring constantly, until sauce thickens and bubbles.

3. Remove from heat and stir in butter, lemon zest and juice. Cool.

4. This makes about 1-1/2 cups. This is great on Thanksgiving/Christmas Carrot pudding.

OLD BOTTLED FRUIT CAKE

Gwen Chesley

4 cups flour (GF mix & 2 tsp. Xanthan)

2 cups sugar

1 cup oil

1 tsp. salt

4 tsp. cinnamon

2 tsp. nutmeg

1 tsp. cloves

4 tsp. soda

1 quart of fruit puree (peaches, pears, or apricots; juice & all blended up)

Nuts and raisins -- optional

1. In a large bowl, mix all dry ingredients except nuts and raisins.
2. Blend the quart of fruit until smooth.
3. Stir into the dry ingredients. Add nuts or raisins, if desired.
4. Pour into a greased and floured 9 x 13 baking dish and bake at 325 degrees for 1 hour.
5. A good way to use up old, darkened fruit that is still good.
6. Frost with Icing for Old Bottled Fruit Cake.

ICING FOR OLD BOTTLED FRUIT CAKE

4 Tbs. butter

1/2 cup brown sugar

1/4 cup evaporated canned milk

2-1/2 cups powdered sugar.

1. Bring to a boil: 4 Tbs. butter, 1/2 cup brown sugar and 1/4 cup canned milk.
2. Add 2-1/2 cups powdered sugar and mix. Frost the cake.

CARROT CAKE

4 eggs

1-1/2 cups oil

2 cups sugar

2 cups flour (GF mix & 1 tsp. Xanthan)

2 tsp. cinnamon

3 cups grated carrots

2 tsp. baking powder (2-1/2 tsp.)

1-1/2 cup chopped nuts

1 tsp. soda

Pinch of salt

1. Beat eggs and add oil.   Add sugar and mix.

2. Whisk together the dry ingredients. Add all dry ingredients and mix.

3. Add carrots and nuts and combine.

4. Bake at 350 degrees for 30 minutes in 2 round 8-9 inch greased, floured, and lined with wax paper pans.

5. Remove from layer pans immediately. Remove waxed paper. Cool on a wire rack.

6. Frost with Cream Cheese Frosting. Keep cake refrigerated after.

CREAM CHEESE FROSTING

1 (3-ounce) package cream cheese

1/2 cup butter

1 tsp. vanilla

3 cups powdered sugar

1. Cream together: 1 (3-ounce) package cream cheese and 1/2 c. butter

2. Add: 1 tsp. vanilla and about 3 cups powdered sugar and mix to spreading consistency.

3. Frost cake and enjoy! This frosting needs to be refrigerated when storing cake.

SUPER MOIST CHOCOLATE CAKE

Julie Chapman

1 (2-layer) chocolate cake mix (use a GF one)

2 cups water

1 large pkg. instant chocolate pudding (GF)

3 eggs

Cherry pie filling (optional)

Chocolate frosting or Chocolate cream frosting, below

1. Mix the above except the cherry pie filling and frosting, and bake as directed on box in   a 9 x 13 baking dish or Bundt pan.

2. Top with your choice of either: plain chocolate frosting, cream frosting; below, or Cherry pie filling

CHOCOLATE CREAM FROSTING

1 large pkg. of instant chocolate pudding, prepared to package directions

1 (8-ounce) tub of frozen whipped topping

1. Mix 1 large pkg. prepared chocolate pudding with 1 tub of cool whip.

2. Frost

PINEAPPLE UPSIDE-DOWN CAKE

1/2 cup butter

1 cup brown sugar

12 canned pineapple rings (from 1 (20-oz.) and 1 (8-oz.) cans)

2 cups flour (GF mix & 1 tsp. Xanthan)

2 tsp. baking powder

1/2 tsp. salt

1/2 tsp. nutmeg

1/2 cup butter; softened

1/2 cup sugar

1/2 cup brown sugar

1/2 cup reserved pineapple juice

2 eggs

1/2 cup milk

1 tsp. vanilla

Whipped cream

12 maraschino cherries

1. Heat oven to 350 degrees. Butter 9x13 pan & line with parchment.

2. Melt 1/2 cup butter, stir in brown sugar. Bring to a boil and pour into pan.

3. In a bowl, whisk dry ingredients. In another bowl, beat soft butter, sugar, and brown sugar for 2 minutes.

4. Add eggs & mix. Beat in half of flour mix. Mix in 1/2 cup pineapple juice and milk. Add rest of flour and vanilla and mix in.

5. Spread batter in pan over pineapple. Bake 35-40 minutes or until toothpick is clean. Cool in pan on rack for 10 minutes. (If you invert too soon, the pineapple may stick to pan.) Invert on a serving tray.

6. Serve warm with whipped cream and a cherry. This can store at room temp. for up to 3 days. Serves 12

CREME OF COCONUT CAKE

1 box yellow butter cake mix (use GF yellow mix and 1 tsp. butter extract flavoring)

1 can of crème of coconut

1 can sweetened condensed Eagle Brand milk

8 oz. Cool Whip

1 pkg. frozen coconut (thawed)

1. Mix and bake yellow butter cake mix by directions on box in 13x9x2 baking dish.

2. While cake is hot, pierce with fork. Combine can of crème of coconut and can of Eagle Brand milk and pour over cake. Cover and refrigerate.

3. When cake is cool, spread with 8 ounces of Cool Whip and a package of frozen coconut (thawed). Store the cake in the refrigerator.

CHOCOLATE PUDDING CAKE

1/2 cup sugar, plus extra to coat the baking dish

6 large eggs, separated

6 ounces semi-sweet chocolate, melted

1/2 tsp. salt

Butter for dish

Powdered sugar to dust top

1. Preheat oven to 350 degrees and set a kettle of water on to boil. Butter a 2 qt. baking dish and coat with granulated sugar.

2. In a bowl, whisk egg yolks with sugar until light in color and then add melted chocolate.

3. In a large bowl, with mixer on high, beat the egg whites with salt until soft peaks form.

4. Whisk 1/3 of egg whites into chocolate mixture and then add the rest.

5. Transfer to prepared dish. Set in a roasting pan and add boiling water to about 1-inch up the side of dish.

6. Bake 25-35 minutes; remove. Dust with powdered sugar just before serving.

BANANA CAKE

1/4 cup flour (GF mix)

1/4 cup brown sugar

1/4 cup butter

2 cups flour (GF mix & 1 tsp. Xanthan)

1-1/2 tsp. baking powder

1 tsp. baking soda

3/4 tsp. salt

3/4 cup sugar

1/2 cup butter, melted

1/2 cup buttermilk

2 eggs

1 tsp. vanilla

2 mashed banana (1 cup)

1. Mix the topping: 1/4 cup flour, 1/4 cup brown sugar and 1/4 cup butter and set aside.

2. Preheat oven to 300 degrees. Combine dry ingredients in a large bowl. Blend in melted butter and add 1/4 cup buttermilk.

3. In another bowl, combine the other 1/4 cup buttermilk and eggs. Pour and blend into flour mixture. Add vanilla and bananas and mix 1 minute.

4. Pour into greased 9x13 baking dish. Top with reserved topping.

5. Bake 35-40 minutes or until a toothpick when inserted comes out clean.

PEAR BATTER CAKE

1/4 cup melted unsalted butter

3 Comice or Bartlett pears

3/4 cup milk

1/3 cup sugar

1/3 cup flour (GF mix & 1/8 tsp. Xanthan)

2 tsp. vanilla

3 large eggs

1/4 tsp. salt

Powdered sugar, for dusting

1. Preheat oven to 350 degrees and butter 9-inch pie plate. Peel, halve, core pears & slice 1/4-inch thick. Arrange in baking dish in a circular pattern.

2. Blend butter, milk, sugar, flour, vanilla, eggs & salt

3. Pour batter over pears. Bake until golden and firm to touch, 40-45 minutes.

   Serve warm, dusted with powdered sugar.

LIBBY'S PUMPKIN ROLL WITH CREAM CHEESE FILLING

Cake:

Powdered sugar

3/4 cup flour (GF mix & 1/2 tsp. Xanthan)

1/2 tsp. baking powder

1/2 tsp. baking soda

1/2 tsp. cinnamon

1/2 tsp. cloves

1/4 tsp. salt

3 large eggs

1 cup sugar

2/3 cup Libby's pumpkin

1 cup chopped walnuts-optional

Filling:

1 pkg. (8 oz.) cream cheese, softened

1 cup sifted powdered sugar

6 Tbs. butter, softened

1 tsp. vanilla

Powdered sugar

1. Preheat oven to 375 degrees. Grease a 16x10-inch jelly roll pan and line with wax paper. Grease and flour the paper. Sprinkle a non-terry kitchen towel with powdered sugar and set aside.

2. Combine dry ingredients in a bowl. Beat eggs and sugar in large mixer bowl until thick. Beat in pumpkin and then stir in flour mixture. Spread evenly into prepared pan and sprinkle with nuts if desired.

3. Bake for 13-15 minutes or until top springs back when touched. Remove.

4. Immediately loosen and turn cake onto prepared towel. Carefully peel away paper. Roll up cake and towel together starting with the narrow end. Cool on wire rack.

5. Beat cream cheese, powdered sugar, butter and vanilla until smooth. Carefully unroll cake; remove towel. Spread cream cheese mixture over cake. Reroll cake.

6. Wrap in plastic and refrigerate at least 1 hour. Sprinkle with powdered sugar before serving. Serves 10

POOR MAN'S FRUIT CAKE

I make this with gumdrops --- Herma (Grandma) Smith's recipe

1 lb. (3 cups) raisins

3 cups of water

1 tsp. soda

2 cups brown sugar

1 cup shortening

2 eggs

3/4 cup molasses or orange juice

4 cups flour (use GF mix & 2 tsp. Xanthan)

1 tsp. nutmeg

1/2 tsp. salt

1 tsp. cinnamon

1/2 tsp. cloves

1 cup chopped nuts

1 pkg. fruit mix or cut-up gumdrops

Glaze:

1/2 cup white corn syrup

1/2 cup water

1. Boil raisins until dry in 3 cups water. Add 1 tsp. soda after they are dry and let cool.

2. Cream the brown sugar and shortening. Add eggs, molasses or orange juice and mix.

3. Add in the dry ingredients and combine. Fold in the fruit mix or gumdrops and nuts.

4. Line loaf pans with wax paper or foil. Bake at 250 degrees for 1 hour and then 300 degrees for 1 hour. Place a pan of water in oven as they bake for moisture. Cool. Yield: 3 loaves

5. *Glaze* for top: Boil for 1 minute 1/2 cup white Karo syrup and 1/2 cup water. Brush on the tops of the loaves; let dry. These are best cured in refrigerator (wrapped) for 2-3 weeks.

FLOURLESS CHOCOLATE CAKE--#1

6 Tbs. unsalted butter

1-1/2 cups semi-sweet chocolate chips

6 large egg yolks

6 large egg whites

1/2 cup sugar

Powdered sugar

1. Preheat oven to 275 degrees with oven rack in center. Butter a 9-inch spring-form pan.

2. Place butter and chocolate in a large bowl. Microwave in 30-second increments; stirring each time, until melted. Cool slightly and whisk in yolks.

3. In another bowl, beat egg whites to soft peaks. Gradually add sugar, beat until stiff and glossy. Whisk 1/4 of whites into chocolate mixture. Gently fold in rest of whites.

4. Pour into prepared pan; smooth top. Bake until cake pulls away from sides of pan and just set in center, 45-50 minutes. Cool completely on wire rack. Unmold. Serve dusted with powdered sugar.

FLOURLESS CHOCOLATE CAKE--#2

1 cup butter; cut into pieces

5 large eggs

1/4 cup cocoa plus extra to dust the pan

1 cup sugar

1-1/4 cup heavy cream

1/2 cup sour cream

8 ounces *bittersweet* chocolate, chopped (1-1/2 c.)

1/4 cup powdered sugar plus extra to dust the cake

1. Heat oven to 350 degrees and butter a 9-inch springform pan and dust with cocoa powder.

2. In a saucepan, heat butter and 1/4 cup cream over medium-low heat until butter is melted. Add the chocolate and stir until melted and smooth; remove from heat.

3. In a bowl, whisk eggs, sugar, and cocoa and whisk it into chocolate mix.

4. Transfer to pan and bake until puffed and set, 35-40 minutes. Let cool in pan for 1 hour. Unmold.

5. Beat the remaining 1 cup of cream and sour cream with powdered sugar until soft peaks form. Dust cake with powdered sugar and serve with cream. (Can be made 2 days ahead and refrigerated.)

LEMON BUNDT POUND CAKE

I have made this every year since 1973 since Travis' First Birthday!

1 pkg. Duncan Hines Moist Lemon Supreme Cake Mix and 1/2 cup flour (Use GF 2 layer yellow cake mix & GF flour plus zest of 1 lemon and juice of 1-2 lemons)

1 package (4 serving size) lemon instant pudding mix (use GF)

4 eggs

1-1/2 cup water

1/4 cup oil

Glaze:

1-1/2 cups powdered sugar

3 Tbs. lemon juice

1. Preheat oven to 375 degrees. Grease and flour a 10-inch Bundt pan or tube pan.

2. Combine cake mix, flour, pudding, eggs, water and oil and beat for 4 minutes in a Bosch or other mixer. Pour into pan and bake for 45-50 minutes. Cool in pan for 25 minutes and then invert on serving plate.

3. *Glaze:* Make a thin frosting with 1-1/2 cups powdered sugar and 3 Tbs. lemon juice. Glaze the cake if desired.

4. *Variation:* Use a yellow cake mix and add in 3 Tbs. poppy seeds, 1 large pkg. vanilla pudding mix, and mix with the other ingredients as above. Grease Bundt pan and then sprinkle in cinnamon-sugar on the sides. Pour half of cake mix in pan, sprinkle with more cinnamon sugar, and top with rest of cake mix. Bake 350 degrees for 35-45 minutes.

MEYER LEMON CREPE CAKE (MARTHA STEWART MAGAZINE-APRIL 2010)

Crepes:

3/4 cup flour (GF mix & 1/2 tsp. Xanthan)

1/2 cup sugar

1/4 tsp. salt

1-1/4 cup whole milk-room temperature

3 eggs, room temperature

1/2 Tbs. vanilla

6 Tbs. cold unsalted butter, melted plus more for pan

Lemon Curd – recipe (p.141) below or use your store bought favorite

1 cup whipped cream to add to the Lemon Curd

1. *Make Crepes*: Whisk together flour, sugar, and salt. Whisk milk, eggs, and vanilla. Gradually pour milk mixture into flour mixture, whisking until smooth. Whisk in melted butter. Pour through a fine sieve into an airtight container, discard lumps. Refrigerate at least 2 hours or overnight.

2. Lightly coat a 6-inch crepe pan or nonstick skillet with butter. Heat pan over medium heat until just starting to smoke. Remove from heat; pour about 2 Tbs. batter into center. Swirl to cover bottom. Reduce heat to medium-low; return pan to heat. Cook until edges are golden and center is dry, about 30 seconds per side.

3. Slide crepe onto an overturned plate. Repeat with remaining batter, coating the pan with butter as needed; and stacking crepes. Let cool.

4. *Make the Lemon curd*: Make the recipe below and whip the cream.

5. *Note:* Make the lemon curd into *lemon curd mousse* from the recipe by just adding 1 cup of cream, whipped, into the curd. Refrigerate this for 1 hour before using.

6. *To Assemble the Crepe Cake:*

7. Place 1 crepe on a flat serving dish. Spread about 1/4 cup lemon curd mousse onto crepe. Top with 1 crepe. Continue layering crepes and mousse, ending with a crepe on top. (this uses 15 crepes) Just a caution: the crepe cake tends to slip to the side if too much Lemon Mousse is added. Refrigerate 1 hour until firm.

8. Top Crepe Cake with additional whipped cream and 3-4 candied lemon slices.

LEMON CURD

2 cups sugar

1 cup fresh lemon juice (about 6 lemons)

4 large eggs, plus 4 large yolks, beaten

1/4 cup finely grated lemon peel (about 3 lemons)

1-1/2 sticks unsalted butter, cut into pieces

1. Set a fine-mesh strainer over a medium heatproof bowl next to the stove. In a heavy saucepan, whisk together the sugar, lemon juice, eggs, yolk, and lemon peel. Add the butter and cook over medium-low heat, stirring constantly for 5 minutes.

2. Lower the heat and simmer, stirring until the mixture thickens and registers 160 degrees on an instant read thermometer, about 5 minutes.

3. Strain the mixture into prepared bowl; then press a sheet of plastic wrap directly onto the surface. Let cool to room temperature. Transfer to an airtight container and refrigerate for up to a month.

OTHER WAYS TO USE THE CURD
- ✓ *spread on English Muffins or toast,*
- ✓ *stir into plain yogurt,*
- ✓ *use as a crepe filling or*
- ✓ *use for the stacked lemon crepe cake*
- ✓ *serve with pancakes and French toast*
- ✓ *fold into whipped cream*
- ✓ *make lemon chicken*

ANNETTE'S CRANBERRY UPSIDE-DOWN COFFEE CAKE

Cake:

1 cup fresh cranberries

1/2 cup coarsely chopped pitted dates

2 Tbs. chopped walnuts

1 tsp. grated orange rind

1/2 cup butter, softened and divided

1/2 cup brown sugar

2 Tbs. fresh orange juice

1/4 tsp. cinnamon

1 tsp. baking powder

1-1/2 cup flour (GF mix & 3/4 tsp. Xanthan)

1 tsp. baking powder

1/2 tsp. salt

1 cup sugar

1 tsp. vanilla

1 large egg

1/2 cup buttermilk

Glaze:

1 cup powdered sugar

1 tsp. butter, melted

2 Tbs. fresh orange juice

1. Preheat oven to 350 degrees.

2. Coat a 9-inch square pan with cooking spray, dust with 1 Tbs. flour (GF). Combine cranberries, dates, walnuts, and rind in a bowl; set aside.

3. Melt 2 Tbs. butter in a small pan and stir in brown sugar, 2 Tbs. orange juice, and cinnamon; cook 3 minutes, stirring constantly. Pour the brown sugar mixture into prepared pan. Sprinkle with cranberry mixture evenly.

4. Lightly spoon 1-1/2 cups flour into dry measuring cups; level with knife. Combine all dry ingredients in a bowl and whisk well.

5. Place sugar and remaining butter in bowl and mix with a mixer. Add vanilla and egg and beat; add buttermilk and flour mixture and blend in. Spoon the batter over cranberry mixture.

6. Bake at 350 degrees for 40 minutes or until wooden toothpick comes out clean in the center. Cool in pan for 5 minutes on a wire rack. Run a knife around the edges and then invert cake onto a serving plate; cool.

7. To prepare glaze, combine all ingredients and stir until smooth. Drizzle over cake. Cut into 12 squares.

GLAZED LEMON POUND CAKE

Makes 2 loaves

1 cup unsalted butter, softened

3 cups flour (use GF mix & 1-1/2 tsp. Xanthan)

3/4 cup buttermilk

1/3 cup lemon juice and zest of 2 lemons

1-1/2 tsp. salt

1/2 tsp. baking powder

1/2 tsp. baking soda

2 cups sugar

5 large eggs

Lemon Glaze - recipe follows

1. Preheat oven to 350 degrees with rack in lowest position. Butter and flour the loaf pans.

2. Combine buttermilk, lemon zest, and juice. Whisk together the dry ingredients in a bowl.

3. Cream the butter and sugar until light and fluffy. Add eggs one at a time, beating after each one.

4. Add flour mixture in 3 parts alternating with buttermilk mixture. Beat just until smooth. Do not over mix. Divide batter between 2 pans and smooth tops.

5. Bake until toothpick comes clean, 50-60 minutes. (Tent with foil if browns too quickly.) Cool in pans 15 minutes and then turn out.

6. *Lemon Glaze:* Add 3 Tbs. lemon juice to 1-1/2 cups powdered sugar and stir until smooth.

7. *To Glaze:* Set rack with cakes over a baking sheet lined with waxed paper. Pour glaze over, letting it run down sides. Let dry 30 minutes.

8. This batter can also be cooked in a 12-cup buttered and floured Bundt pan. Cooking time is the same.

ANNETTE'S POPPY SEED CAKE

1 (2 layer) yellow cake mix (use GF)

1 pkg. French Vanilla Instant Pudding (GF)

4 eggs

1 cup sour cream

1/2 cup water

1 tsp. almond extract

1/4 cup poppy seeds

1. To 1 yellow cake mix (use GF mix), add: 1 package instant French Vanilla Pudding (GF), 4 eggs, 1 cup sour cream, 1/2 cup water, 1 tsp. almond extract, and 1/4 cup poppy seeds.

2. Mix and put into a greased and floured (GF flour) Bundt pan.

3. Bake at 350 degrees for 45 minutes. Serve with cream, strawberries and a sprig of peppermint, if desired.

CHOCOLATE TEXAS SHEET CAKE

Makes a 12x18 sheet cake-----Heat oven to 350 degrees.

Cake:

2 cups flour (GF mix & 1 tsp. Xanthan)

2 cups sugar

1/4 tsp. salt

1/2 cup buttermilk

2 large eggs

1 tsp. vanilla

1 tsp. baking soda

1/2 lb. (2 sticks) butter

4 heaping Tbs. cocoa powder

Icing:

1-3/4 sticks butter

4 heaping Tbs. cocoa powder

6 Tbs. milk

1 tsp. vanilla

1 lb. powdered sugar

1/2 cup finely chopped pecans

1. In a large bowl, combine flour, sugar and salt. In another bowl, mix buttermilk, vanilla, eggs, and soda

2. In a medium saucepan, melt butter and cocoa; mix. Boil 1 cup of water & add to cocoa mix. Turn off heat. Pour chocolate mixture into flour mix. Stir to cool. Pour into egg mixture and stir until smooth.

3. Pour into sheet cake pan. Bake 20 minutes at 350 degrees until toothpick is clean.

4. Make Icing While Cake Is Baking: Melt butter, add cocoa and stir until smooth. Add milk, vanilla and powdered sugar; stir. Add nuts.

5. Immediately after cake is out of oven pour over icing.

FOURLESS CHOCOLATE CAKE OR CUPCAKES

6 Tbs. (3/4 stick) unsalted butter

8 ounces bittersweet chocolate coarsely chopped (or 1-1/2 cup semisweet chocolate chips)

6 large eggs, separated, room temperature

1/2 cup sugar

1. Preheat oven to 275 degrees. Line standard muffin tins with paper liners or butter a 9-inch springform pan.

2. Melt butter and chocolate in a large heatproof bowl set over (not in) a pan of simmering water. Stir to combine, then remove bowl from heat and let cool slightly. Whisk in egg yolks.

3. With an electric mixer on medium speed, whisk egg whites until soft peaks form. Gradually add sugar, beating until peaks are stiff and glossy, but not dry (do not overbeat). Whisk one quarter of the beaten egg whites into chocolate mixture; and then gently fold mixture into remaining whites.

4. Divide batter evenly among the lined cups (22), filling each 3/4 full or in the springform pan.

5. Bake; rotating tins halfway through, until cupcakes are just set in centers, about 25 minutes. Bake the springform pan 45-50 minutes until the cake pulls away from sides of the pan.

6. Transfer tins to wire rack to cool completely before removing cupcakes (their centers will sink). Dust lightly with powdered sugar. Best eaten the same day they are baked. Keep at room temperature. Serve with a scoop of ice cream or dust with powdered sugar.

TRES LECHES CAKE

1 cup white flour (use GF mix and 1/2 tsp. Xanthan)

1-1/2 tsp. baking powder

5 whole large eggs, separated

1 tsp. vanilla

1 can (11.5 oz.) of evaporated milk

1/4 tsp. salt

1 cup sugar, divided

1/3 cup milk

1 can sweetened condensed milk

1/4 cup heavy cream

Frosting:

1 pint heavy cream, whipped

3 Tbs. powdered sugar

1. Preheat oven to 350 degrees. Spray a 9 x 13 baking pan liberally.

2. Combine flour, baking powder, and salt in a large bowl.

3. Separate eggs. Beat the egg yolks with 3/4 cup sugar on High speed until the yolks are pale yellow in color. Stir in milk and vanilla; mix again.

4. Pour egg yolk mixture over the flour mixture and stir very gently until well combined.

5. Beat egg whites on High speed until you have soft peaks. With the mixer on, pour in remaining 1/4 cup sugar and beat until egg whites are stiff, but not dry.

6. Fold egg white mixture into the batter very gently.

7. Pour into the pan and spread evenly. Bake for 35 to 45 minutes. Remove.

8. After cake has slightly cooled, gently poke holes throughout the cake with a fork.

9. Mix together the evaporated milk, condensed milk and 1/4 cup heavy cream.

10. Pour over the cake and let it soak in.

11. Make frosting by whipping the cream and adding in 3 Tbs. powdered sugar.

12. Frost the cake and sprinkle the top with cinnamon. Refrigerate until it has cooled to allow milk to soak in before serving.

GLUTEN FREE YELLOW CAKE (OIL-BASED)

1-1/2 cups Featherlight mix, p.271

1/2 tsp. xanthan gum

3/4 cup sugar

1/2 tsp. salt

2 tsp. baking powder

3/4 cup vanilla yogurt

2 tsp. vanilla

1/4 cup oil

1 lightly beaten egg

1. Preheat oven to 350 degrees. Grease an 8-inch square pan.

2. Combine Featherlight mix, xanthan gum, sugar, salt, and baking powder. In a separate bowl, combine yogurt, vanilla, oil, and egg.

3. Add to dry ingredients. Beat for 2 minutes. Pour into pan.

4. Bake 30 minutes, until a toothpick inserted in center of cake comes out clean.

CHOCOLATE PEPPERMINT BUNDT CAKE

Cocoa powder for dusting pan

1 box Devil's Food Cake mix (I prefer Duncan Hines) - (Use a GF cake mix)

1 small box instant chocolate pudding

4 eggs

1 cup full fat sour cream

1 cup oil

1/2 cup milk

1 teaspoon vanilla extract

2 teaspoons peppermint extract

3/4 to 1 cup dark chocolate chips, roughly chopped

Glaze:

1/2 cup dark chocolate chips

1/2 Tbs. butter

1/2 cup cream

1/2 teaspoon peppermint extract

Additional ingredients:

2 Crushed candy canes

For serving:

Whipped cream or ice cream

for extra peppermint-y goodness, add a little peppermint extract to your sweetened whipped cream while whipping

1. Preheat oven to 350 degrees. Butter a Bundt pan (make sure to get the inside center as well) and then dust with cocoa powder, covering all sides and then shaking out excess.

2. Place cake mix and dry pudding mix in the bowl of a stand mixer. In a small mixing bowl, whisk together eggs, sour cream, oil, milk, vanilla, and peppermint until smooth. With mixer running, add liquid ingredients to cake mix and beat until combined. Scrape down sides of bowl and then beat for 2 minutes on medium high speed. Add chocolate chips and stir until combined. Pour batter into Bundt pan and bake for 45-50 minutes, until a skewer comes out with moist crumbs attached.

3. *Glaze*: While cake is baking, place chocolate chips and butter in a bowl. Heat cream until hot and bubbly and then pour over chocolate. Let sit for 2-3 minutes, then add peppermint and whisk until smooth. Set aside.

4. When cake is done, let cool until just warm (15-20 minutes). Invert the cake onto a paper towel on a metal rack. Let cool completely and place on serving platter. To glaze cake: Use either a brush to lightly brush chocolate over the surface, or use a spoon and drizzle the chocolate over. You may have extra. If too thick, heat for a few seconds to loosen, if still warm and too runny, let cool longer or place in fridge to speed up process.

5. After cake is glazed (and you may want to wait for the glaze to set just a bit), sprinkle with crushed candy canes. Slice into servings and serve with a dollop of whipped cream or vanilla ice cream.

FANCY CUPCAKES

Tiffany Magleby

COOKIES & CREAM CUPCAKES

Triple chocolate cake mix (use a GF mix)

1 small box instant chocolate pudding

1 cup milk

Buttercream frosting

Marshmallow Crème topping

Crushed Oreo cookies (use GF)

1. Make according to cake mix instructions plus add 1 small box instant chocolate pudding and 1 cup milk. Fill paper-lined muffin cups about 1/2 full and bake according to cake mix instructions.

2. Using a Wilton 230 tip, fill cupcakes with a mixture of Buttercream frosting and Marshmallow topping. Use about 1/2 of each combined together.

3. Frost cupcakes using a Wilton 1M tip with Buttercream frosting, p. 153.

4. Top with crushed Oreo cookies (use GF cookies).

LEMON RASPBERRY CUPCAKES

1 Lemon cake mix (use a GF cake mix)

Plain yogurt

Raspberry pie filling

Whipped cream

1. Make the Lemon cake mix (use GF mix--if can't find a lemon cake mix, use a yellow mix with zest and juice of 1-2 lemons). Make according to the box instructions but substitute the same measurement of yogurt for oil.

2. Fill paper-lined muffin cups about 1/2 full of batter and bake according to cake mix instructions.

3. Using a Wilton 230 tip and a bag, fill cupcakes with Raspberry pie filling.

4. Whip Cream with mixer, adding a little sugar to sweeten. Fold in some raspberry pie filling. Frost the cupcakes using a Wilton 1M with the whipped cream mixture. (Frost cupcakes close to serving time.) Top with a raspberry.

LINDT TRUFFLE CHOCOLATE CUPCAKES

1 box devil's food cake mix (use GF)

1 small box instant vanilla pudding (GF)

4 eggs

1/2 cup oil

1/2 cup water

1 cup sour cream

24 Milk Chocolate Lindor Truffles

1. Unwrap truffles; set aside. Mix all cupcake ingredients together. Blend with mixer for 30 seconds; then mix for 2 minutes. Fill the paper-liners with batter about 2/3 full.

2. Bake at 350 degrees. After 5 minutes of baking, press a truffle into the center of each cupcake. Bake an additional 13 minutes.

3. Cool completely, then frost with cream cheese frosting using the Wilton 1M tip.

CHOCOLATE PEANUT BUTTER CUPCAKES

Triple chocolate cake mix (use GF mix)

1 small box instant chocolate pudding mix

1 cup milk

Filling:

1/2 cup butter

1/2 cup peanut butter

1 cup crushed graham cracker crumbs (GF)

1 cup powdered sugar

1. Make cupcakes according to cake mix instructions plus adding 1 small box instant chocolate pudding and 1 cup milk.

2. Fill paper-lined muffin cups about 1/2 full. Bake according to cake mix instructions.

3. *For the filling*: Put peanut butter and butter in glass bowl and microwave for approx. 45 seconds or until melted. Stir together and add graham crumbs and powdered sugar. Mix together. Refrigerate for 20-30 minutes.

4. Spoon out the center of the cupcake. Roll filling into a ball and place in the center of the cupcake.

5. Frost with Buttercream frosting (p.153) with a little added cocoa powder using the 1 M Wilton tip.

6. Top with cut up Reese's Peanut Butter Cups.

CREAM CHEESE FROSTING FOR CUPCAKES

Great for Fancy Cupcakes!

1/2 cup butter

8 oz. cream cheese

1/2 tsp. vanilla

3 cups powdered sugar

1. Cream the butter and cream cheese. Add vanilla. Mix in powdered sugar.

2. If desired, you can add cocoa powder to make the frosting chocolaty.

3. Frost cupcakes using the 1M Wilton tip or frost any other cake, as desired.

BUTTERCREAM CUPCAKE FROSTING

Use this with margarine for cupcake frosting

1/2 stick or (4 Tbs.) <u>margarine</u> (works best when margarine is room temperature)

2-1/2 cups powdered sugar

1/4 tsp. salt

1 tsp. vanilla

4 Tbsp. cream

1. Combine ingredients and blend with mixer until firm enough to hold shape.

2. *Double or triple this recipe* for each cupcake mix you are making. This uses a lot of frosting and it's such a pain to go back and make more if you run out.

CUPCAKE DECORATING TIPS TO USE

Use a Wilton 230 tip to fill the cupcakes

Use a Wilton 1M tip to frost the cupcakes.

FROSTINGS

SOFT ELEVEN MINUTE FROSTING

Bernice Gundry

1 cup sugar

1 cup water

1 cup white corn syrup

2 stiffly beaten egg whites

1/4 tsp. cream of tartar

1. Bring to a boil on high, then turn to med. high and cook for 11 minutes: 1 cup sugar, 1 cup water and 1 cup white corn syrup.

2. Pour slowly into 2 stiffly beaten egg whites and add 1/4 tsp. cream of tartar. Beat until thick.

3. Frost the cake.

COOKED FROSTING

1 cup sugar

1/3 cup water

1/4 tsp. cream of tartar

Dash salt

2 unbeaten egg whites

1 tsp. vanilla

1. Bring to a boil; cook until sugar dissolves: 1 cup sugar, 1/3 cup water, 1/4 tsp. cream of tartar, and a dash of salt

2. Slowly add syrup to 2 unbeaten egg whites. Beat 7 minutes until peaks form. Add 1 tsp. vanilla. Frost the cake.

CREAM CHEESE FROSTING FOR CAKES

1 (3-ounce) package cream cheese

1/2 cup butter

1 tsp. vanilla

3 cups powdered sugar

1. Cream together: 1 (3-ounce) package cream cheese and 1/2 cup butter

2. Add: 1 tsp. vanilla and about 3 cups powdered sugar and mix to spreading consistency.

3. Frost cake and enjoy! This frosting needs to be refrigerated when storing cake.

QUICK CARAMEL FROSTING

1/2 cup butter

1/2 cup brown sugar

1/4 cup milk

1-3/4 cup powdered sugar

1 tsp. vanilla

1. Melt 1/2 cup butter; and then add 1/2 cup brown sugar and 1/4 cup milk. Stir until sugar melts. Remove and cool.

2. Beat in 1-3/4 cup or more powdered sugar, a little at a time until thick enough to spread. Add 1 tsp. vanilla and blend in. Frost the cake.

HERSHEY'S 5-MINUTE CHOCOLATE FROSTING

6 Tbs. butter

2-2/3 cups powdered sugar

1/2 cup cocoa

4-5 Tbs. milk

1 Tbs. vanilla

1. Cream butter until soft; add cocoa and blend.

2. Add powdered sugar with milk and vanilla and beat to spreading consistency.

3. Makes 2 cups (enough to frost a layer cake or 2-1/2 dozen cupcakes)

CHOCOLATE FROSTING

1/4 cup hot water

2 Tbs. butter

1/2 tsp. vanilla

2 Tbs. cocoa

2 cups powdered sugar

1. Heat on stove: 1/4 cup hot water, 2 Tbs. butter, and 1/2 tsp. vanilla. Add 2 Tbs. cocoa; stir.

2. Remove from heat; add 2 cups powdered sugar and beat until good consistency. Frost

GERMAN CHOCOLATE CAKE FROSTING

1 cup sugar

3 slightly beaten egg yolks

1 cup evaporated canned milk

1/2 cup butter

1 tsp. vanilla

1-1/3 cups coconut

1 cup chopped pecans

1. Combine and cook and stir over medium heat until thickened (about 12 min.): 1 cup sugar, 3 slightly beaten egg yolks, 1 cup canned milk, 1/2 cup butter, and 1 tsp. vanilla.

2. Remove from heat and add 1-1/3 cups coconut and 1 cup chopped pecans. Cool until mixture is spreading consistency; beating occasionally. Covers 2-3 layers

ABSOLUTELY DIVINE CHOCOLATE FROSTING

Frosts a layer cake or 2 (9x13) pans

2 cups whipping cream

1 tsp. vanilla

24 ounces semi-sweet chocolate chips

1. Heat the cream in a pan over medium heat until just boiling. Reduce to low and add chocolate and 1 tsp. vanilla. Stir until smooth.

2. Chill in refrigerator in a glass bowl, stirring every 10 minutes until consistency of pudding. Continue to chill, stirring every 5 minutes until consistency of fudge. Let stand at room temp until spreading consistency.

3. Frost the cake and stand at room temp to set. Refrigerate after set before serving.

BUTTERCREAM FROSTING WITH VARIATIONS

3-3/4 cups - (1 lb. box) powdered sugar

1/2 cup - butter (1 stick), softened

3 to 4 tablespoons - milk

1 teaspoon - vanilla extract

1. In a large bowl with electric mixer at low speed, combine sugar, butter, milk and vanilla.

2. Beat at medium speed 1 to 2 minutes until creamy. If desired, add more milk until frosting is spreading consistency.

3. Makes enough to fill and frost a 2-layer cake, a 13x9x2-inch sheet cake or 24 cupcakes.

SUGGESTION
FROSTING VARIATIONS:

4. **Peanut Butter Crunch**—substitute peanut butter for butter; sprinkle either candy peanut butter pieces or chopped peanuts over frosting.

5. **Chocolate**—add 1/3 cup unsweetened cocoa powder to powdered sugar mixture, and add extra milk, a teaspoon at a time until desired consistency. Top with chocolate curls, if desired.

6. **Orange**—substitute fresh orange juice for milk, add 1 tsp. orange extract and 1 tsp. grated orange zest. Top with thin strips of orange peel.

7. **Lemon**--substitute fresh lemon juice for milk, add 1 tsp. lemon extract and 1 tsp. grated lemon zest. Top with thin strips of lemon peel.

8. **Peppermint** --Prepare as directed above, except use 1/2 to 3/4 teaspoon peppermint extract instead of the vanilla. Yield: about 3 cups.

9. **Almond Buttercream Frosting** - Prepare as directed above, use 1/2 to 3/4 teaspoon almond extract instead of the vanilla. Yield: about 3 cups.

STRAWBERRY OR RASPBERRY FILLING FOR WHITE OR CHOCOLATE CAKES

1 small pkg. strawberry/raspberry Jello

1 cup of hot water

1 cup of strawberries/raspberries

1 cup of whipped cream

1. Dissolve 1 small pkg. strawberry/raspberry Jello in 1 cup of hot water. Add 1 cup of strawberries/raspberries and set until medium thick.

2. Add 1 cup of whipped cream. Mix and put between layers of Angel, white, or chocolate cake. Set for 2 hours in refrigerator.

3. You can also frost the top with additional whipped cream or icing and add more strawberries/raspberries to decorate.

COOKIES

BEAUEN'S KILLER CHOCOLATE CHIPS COOKIES

Extra Large Batch!

3 cups shortening – butter flavor is Beau's choice--or use butter

1-1/2 cups brown sugar

3 cups sugar

2 Tbs. vanilla

6 eggs

1 Tbs. baking soda (GF use 1 tsp baking powder too)

2 tsp. salt

6 - 7 cups or up to 8 - 9 cups flour (use GF mix & 3-4 tsp. Xanthan)

2 cups chocolate chips or to taste

1. Cream shortening and sugars; add vanilla and eggs.

2. Add dry ingredients and mix to a good consistency. Add 2 cups chocolate chips; mix in.

3. Drop onto greased baking sheets. Bake at 375 degrees for 10 minutes

JANELLE'S CHOCOLATE CHIP OATMEAL COOKIES

2 cups butter

2 cups sugar

2 cups brown sugar

4 eggs

2 tsp. vanilla

5 cups oatmeal; blended slightly (use GF oats)

4 cups flour (use GF mix & 2 tsp. Xanthan)

1 tsp. salt

2 tsp. baking powder (GF use 2-1/2 tsp.)

2 tsp. baking soda

1 package chocolate chips or to taste

1. Cream butter and sugars. Add the eggs and vanilla and mix.

2. Add in the dry ingredients and mix. Stir in the chocolate chips.

3. Bake at 350 degrees for 12 minutes on greased cookie sheets.

GRANDMA'S SCOTCHEROOS

Our Pond Family Favorite Camping Treat!

1 cup light corn syrup

1 cup sugar

1 cup peanut butter, smooth or crunchy

6 cups Rice Krispie cereal

1 cup semi-sweet chocolate chips

1 cup butterscotch chips

1. In a large pan add the sugar and corn syrup. Heat until the sugar dissolves. Don't boil.

2. Remove from heat and add 1 cup of peanut butter; stir in.

3. Stir in 6 cups Rice Krispies. Spread into a 9x13 pan.

4. Flatten out to make smooth. I always run cold water on my hands and then I can flatten them with my hands without burning them.

5. In a small saucepan: Melt 1 cup butterscotch chips and 1 cup semisweet chocolate chips until smooth. Spread over the top. Let cool! Enjoy!

MRS. FIELDS (COPYCAT) CHOCOLATE CHIP COOKIES

Makes 96 Medium or 72 Large

1 pound butter, melted

1-1/2 cups sugar

2 cups brown sugar

3 eggs

2 Tbs. vanilla

1-1/2 tsp. salt

5-1/2 cups flour (use GF mix & 3 tsp. Xanthan)

1-1/2 tsp. baking soda

6 cups chocolate chips (or 1-1/2 c. raisins and 3/4 cup oats (GF) for Oatmeal cookies)

2 cups chopped nuts, optional

1. Mix together the melted butter and the sugars. Add eggs and vanilla.

2. Add in the dry ingredients and chocolate chips or raisins and oats.

3. Bake at 375 degrees for 10 minutes on greased baking sheet.

SOFT BATCH GLUTEN FREE CHOCOLATE CHIP COOKIES

These are great with chocolate chips, raisins, peanut butter chips, butterscotch chips, chopped Andes mints...etc. Dough freezes great, too.

1 cup butter

3/4 cup packed brown sugar

1/4 cup sugar

1 (3.4 oz.) instant pudding (vanilla or chocolate)

2 eggs

1 tsp. vanilla

2-1/4 cups Featherlight mix (in GF section)--or regular flour for non-GF

1 tsp. xanthan gum (leave out for regular non-GF)

1 tsp. baking soda

1 cup chocolate chips

1 cup nuts (optional)

1. Preheat oven to 350 degrees. Cream butter, sugars, and pudding mix. Add eggs and vanilla and mix in.

2. Whisk flour, xanthan gum and soda; gradually beat into the creamed mixture. Stir in chips and nuts.

3. Drop 2 inches apart on an ungreased baking sheet. Bake 11 minutes. Let Cool.

CHOCOLATE CRINKLE COOKIES

2 cups sugar

1/2 cup butter

4 squares (1 oz. each) baking chocolate; melted (or mix 3/4 cup cocoa & 4 tsp. oil)

4 eggs

2 tsp. vanilla

2 cups flour (use GF mix & 1 tsp. Xanthan)

1/4 tsp. salt

2 tsp. baking powder

3/4 cup powdered sugar

1. Combine sugar and butter and mix well; then add eggs and vanilla and mix. Add in the melted chocolate squares.

2. Combine the flour, salt and baking powder; add to chocolate mixture. Cover and chill 2 hours.

3. Shape into balls and roll in powdered sugar (3/4 cup), coating lightly.

4. Place 2 inches apart on baking sheets. Bake 350 degrees for 14 minutes. Remove and cool.

PEANUT BLOSSOMS

Makes 48

1/2 cup butter or shortening

1/2 cup peanut butter

1/2 cup sugar

1/2 cup brown sugar

1 egg

1-3/4 cups flour (GF use GF mix & 3/4 tsp. Xanthan)

1 tsp. soda

1/2 tsp. salt

2 Tbs. milk

1 tsp. vanilla

48 chocolate kisses

1. Cream the shortening, butters, and sugars. Add egg and mix.

2. Mix dry ingredients and add alternately with milk.

3. Roll into balls and then roll in sugar. Place on baking sheet.

4. Bake at 375 degrees for 12 minutes. Remove; top each cookie with chocolate kiss when hot.

CHEWY OATMEAL COOKIES

Yum! Yum!

1 cup shortening

2 cups brown sugar

1 tsp. vanilla

2 eggs

1 tsp. baking soda

1/4 cup boiling water

2 cups flour (use a GF mix & 1 tsp. Xanthan)

1/2 tsp. salt

2 cups quick oatmeal (use GF)

1. Cream shortening and sugar. Add in the eggs and vanilla; mix well.

2. Dissolve the baking soda in the boiling water and add; mix.

3. Stir in the dry ingredients until blended.

4. Drop onto a greased cookie sheet and bake for 10 minutes at 375 degrees.

LARGE OATMEAL COOKIES

1 cup shortening

1 cup sugar

1/2 cup brown sugar

1 egg

1 tsp. vanilla

1-1/2 cups flour (use GF mix & 3/4 tsp. Xanthan)

1 tsp. soda

1 tsp. cinnamon

1-1/2 cups quick oats (use GF)

3/4 cup chopped nuts (optional)

Sugar and butter for the bottom of the glass to flatten cookies

1. Cream the shortening and sugars. Mix in the egg and vanilla.

2. Add in the 1-1/2 cups flour (use GF mix & 3/4 tsp. Xanthan) 1 tsp. soda, 1 tsp. cinnamon and 1-1/2 cups quick oats. Mix in well. Add in the nuts, if desired, and mix.

3. Chill 1 hour; then roll into walnut to golf ball size balls. Place on a greased cookie sheet.

4. Butter the bottom of a glass and then dip it into sugar. With the glass, press the cookie flat. Dip the glass into the butter and sugar as needed.

5. Bake at 350 degrees for 10 minutes on greased cookie sheet.

SNICKERDOODLES

1 cup butter or shortening

1-1/2 cup sugar

2 eggs

1/2 tsp. vanilla

2-3/4 cups flour (GF use GF mix & 1-1/2 tsp. Xanthan)

2 tsp. cream of tartar

1 tsp. soda (GF use 1-1/2 tsp. soda)

1/4 tsp. salt

3 Tbs. sugar

1 tsp. cinnamon

1. Mix together the 3 Tbs. sugar and 1 tsp. cinnamon and set aside.

2. Cream together the butter or shortening and 1-1/2 cups sugar. Add the eggs and vanilla.

3. Add in the dry ingredients.

4. Roll into small balls and roll in the cinnamon/sugar mixture (3 Tbs. sugar and 1 tsp. cinnamon). Bake at 350 degrees for 8-10 minutes on greased cookie sheet.

CINNAMON-SUGAR RAISIN COOKIES

I love these cookies....could eat a bunch!

1-1/2 cups raisins

1 cup water

1 cup shortening

1-1/3 cups sugar

3 eggs

1 tsp. vanilla

3 cups flour (use GF mix & 1-1/2 tsp. Xanthan)

1 tsp. baking soda (for GF use 1-1/2 tsp.)

3 Tbs. sugar

1 tsp. cinnamon

1. Simmer until dry: 1-1/2 cups raisins and 1 cup water

2. Cream: 1 cup shortening, 1-1/3 cup sugar, 3 eggs, 1 tsp. vanilla

3. Add: 3 cups flour (use GF mix & 1-1/2 tsp. Xanthan), 1 tsp. soda (GF 1-1/2 tsp.)

4. Add the simmered raisins and mix in.

5. Mix in a small bowl the 1/4 cup sugar and 1 tsp. cinnamon.

6. Roll 1 tsp. of dough into a ball and then roll into the cinnamon/sugar mix. Indent slightly with fingertip after putting on greased cookie sheet. Bake at 375 degrees for 10 minutes.

SOFT GINGER SNAPS

Another favorite of mine!

1-1/2 cups oil

2 cups sugar

2 eggs

1/2 cup molasses

4 cups flour (use GF mix & 2 tsp. Xanthan)

4 tsp. soda (GF use 1 tsp. baking powder, also)

1 tsp. salt

2 Tbs. ginger

2 tsp. cinnamon

1/4 cup sugar for rolling the cookies in

1. Mix and set aside: 4 cups flour (use GF mix & 2 tsp. Xanthan), 4 tsp. soda (GF use 1 tsp. baking powder, also), 1 tsp. salt, 2 Tbs. ginger and 2 tsp. cinnamon

2. Blend together: 1-1/2 cup oil, 2 cups sugar, 2 eggs, and 1/2 cup molasses; add the dry ingredients and mix in. Refrigerate dough for 1 hour to chill.

3. Form into balls using 1 tsp. of dough and then roll into the sugar.

4. Bake on ungreased cookie sheet at 350 degrees for 8 minutes. Cool. Makes 4 dozen

MELTING MOMENTS

1/2 pound butter

5-1/2 Tbs. powdered sugar

3/4 cup cornstarch

1 cup flour (use GF mix & 1/2 tsp. Xanthan)

3/4 cup powdered sugar

Milk, to desired consistency for icing

Food color to tint icing, if desired

1. Cream: 1/2 pound butter, 5-1/2 Tbs. powdered sugar, and 3/4 cup cornstarch

2. Add the 1 cup flour (use GF mix & 1/2 tsp. Xanthan) and mix.

3. Roll into balls the size of nickels. Bake at 350 degrees for 20 minutes and cool.

4. Meanwhile, mix the 3/4 cup powdered sugar with just enough milk for a thicker icing.

5. Dot each cookie with the icing. Let set

POWDERED SUGAR COOKIES

Wedding Cookies

1 cup butter

1/2 tsp. salt

4 Tbs. powdered sugar

1 tsp. vanilla

2 cups flour (GF mix & 1 tsp. Xanthan)

1 cup chopped nuts (pecans)

Powdered sugar to roll cookies in

1. Cream: 1 cup butter, 1/2 tsp. salt, and 4 Tbs. powdered sugar

2. Add: 1 tsp. vanilla, 2 cups flour (GF mix & 1 tsp. Xanthan), and 1 cup chopped nuts.

3. Shape into balls or finger shaped cookies and then roll into powdered sugar.

4. Bake at 350 degrees for 8-10 minutes; remove, cool, and then roll again into powdered sugar. These freeze well.

GERMAN BUTTER COOKIES

These can also be used for Irish shortbread cookies.

2 pounds butter

2-1/4 cups sugar

1 Tbs. vanilla (or 5 pkg. Albona Vanillinzucker powder--from a German food store)

7 cups flour (use GF mix & 4 tsp. Xanthan)

1 Tbs. baking powder (GF use 1-1/2 Tbs.)

1/2 pound cornstarch

1. Cream 2 pounds butter and slowly add 2-1/4 cups sugar and 1 Tbs. vanilla (or 5 pkg. Albona Vanillinzucker powder-German store). Beat until fluffy.

2. Whisk 7 cups flour (use GF mix & 4 tsp. Xanthan), 1 Tbs. baking powder (GF use 1-1/2 Tbs.) and 1/2 pound cornstarch and add to the batter slowly.

3. Drop onto ungreased cookie sheet with a cookie gun. Bake at 350 degrees for 10 minutes.

SHORTBREAD COOKIES

1-1/4 cup flour (use a GF mix and 1-1/8 tsp. Xanthan)
1/4 cup sugar
1/2 cup soft butter
1 tsp. vanilla

1. Combine all and mix in butter until crumbly.
2. Pat into an 8 x 8-inch pan.
3. Bake at 325 degrees for 25-30 minutes. The bottom will be brown.
4. Remove and cut into bars before they cool.

ZUCCHINI DROP COOKIES

1 cup sugar
1/2 cup butter (softened)
1 egg
2 cups flour (GF mix & 1 tsp. Xanthan)
1 tsp. soda (GF use 1/2 tsp. baking powder also)
1/2 tsp. cloves
1 tsp. cinnamon
1/2 tsp. salt
1 cup grated zucchini
1 cup raisins or chocolate chips - your choice
1 cup nuts - optional

1. Cream: 1 cup sugar, 1/2 cup butter (softened), and 1 egg until fluffy
2. Whisk dry ingredients together and add. Mix into the creamed mixture well.
3. Add: 1 cup grated zucchini, 1 cup raisins or chocolate chips, and 1 cup nuts
4. Drop on greased cookie sheet and bake at 375 degrees for 12-15 minutes. Makes 3 dozen

172

PUMPKIN COOKIES

1/2 cup shortening

1-1/4 cups brown sugar

2 eggs

1-1/2 cups pumpkin

1/2 tsp. salt

1/4 tsp. ginger

1/2 tsp. nutmeg

1/2 tsp. cinnamon

2-1/2 cups flour (use GF mix & 1-1/4 tsp. Xanthan)

4 tsp. baking powder

1 tsp. lemon extract

1 cup chocolate chips, if desired

1. Cream: 1/2 cup shortening and 1-1/4 cups brown sugar

2. Stir in: 2 eggs and 1-1/2 cups pumpkin

3. Add and mix in the dry ingredients, the lemon extract and chocolate chips.

4. Bake at 400 degrees for 12-15 minutes

EASY PEANUT BUTTER COOKIES

These are flourless yummy cookies --Gluten Free also!

1 cup peanut butter

1 cup white or brown sugar

1 egg

1 tsp. soda

1 tsp. vanilla

1 cup chocolate chips (opt.)

1. Mix the peanut butter sugar, egg, soda, and vanilla together. Stir in chips (optional)

2. Bake at 350 degrees for 8 to 10 minutes on an ungreased pan. These are *tender* cookies when warm. Let cool 5 min. on the cookie sheets before removing.

PINEAPPLE PARTY COOKIES

Bernice Gundry

6 Tbs. butter

1/2 cup sugar

1 egg

1-1/2 cups flour (GF mix & 3/4 tsp. Xanthan)

1/2 tsp. salt

1/2 cup crushed pineapple, not drained

1/4 tsp. soda

1/3 cup finely chopped nuts

Pale green icing - made with powdered sugar, milk, and green food coloring

Finely chopped/blended coconut

1. Cream the 6 Tbs. butter and 1/2 cup sugar; add the egg and mix.

2. Add 1-1/2 cups flour (GF mix & 3/4 tsp. Xanthan), 1/2 tsp. salt and blend.

3. Stir In: 1/2 cup crushed pineapple, not drained with 1/4 tsp. soda added and 1/3 cup nuts

4. Drop on cookie sheets and bake at 350 for 10-12 minutes.

5. When cool, frost with pale green frosting made from powdered sugar, green coloring, and milk. Dip tops in coconut that had been blended fine.

ORANGE DELIGHT COOKIES

Bernice Gundry

3/4 cup shortening

1-1/2 cups brown sugar

2 eggs

1 tsp. orange rind (grated)

1/2 cup buttermilk

1/2 tsp. soda

2 tsp. baking powder

1/2 tsp. salt

3 cups flour (GF mix & 1-1/2 tsp. Xanthan)

1/2 cup pecans

Icing:

1 cup white sugar

1/3 cup orange juice

1 tsp. orange rind

1. Cream: 3/4 cup shortening and 1-1/2 cups brown sugar; add 2 eggs and mix

2. Add: 1 tsp. orange rind (grated) and 1/2 cup buttermilk

3. Add: the dry ingredients; mix. Add the pecans and blend.

4. Bake at 350 degrees until light brown – 10 minutes.

5. Make the icing by combining the sugar, orange juice and rind and let set while baking. Do not cook this icing, only mix it together and let it set.

6. Frost the cookies while still hot. Drizzle on the icing mixture with a teaspoon over the top of each cookie. Place cookies on a rack while icing with a dish under to catch the excess.

GRANDMA SMITH'S RAISIN-FILLED COOKIES

My Favorite Cookies When I Was Young!

Dough: (double this dough for raisin filling recipe p.176)

> **1 cup sugar**
>
> **1/2 cup shortening**
>
> **1 tsp. vanilla**
>
> **1/4 light corn syrup**
>
> **1 tsp. baking powder**
>
> **2 eggs**
>
> **1/2 tsp. salt**
>
> **2-1/2 cup rice flour**
>
> **2/3 cup potato starch**
>
> **1/2 cup tapioca starch**
>
> **1-1/2 tsp. Xanthan**

(For non-GF add 3-2/3 cups flour and no Xanthan, rice flour, potato or tapioca starch)

1. In a large mixing bowl, cream sugar and shortening. Add eggs, corn syrup, and vanilla.

2. In a medium bowl, mix all dry ingredients and then add to the creamed mixture.

3. Divide dough in thirds and shape each part in a roll 8-inches long and 2-inches in diameter. Wrap in plastic wrap and refrigerate at least 4 hours or overnight. Slice cookie rolls in 1/4-inch slices.

4. Place 1 rounded teaspoon of raisin filling (recipe p.176) on the center of each cookie and top with another slice. Press edges together with fingertips.

5. Place on greased cookie sheet. Bake 10-15 minutes at 350 degrees.

NEXT BEST THING TO TOM SELLICK COOKIES

1-1/2 cups brown sugar

3/4 cup butter

2 Tbs. water

1 (12-ounce) package semisweet chocolate chips

2 eggs

2-1/2 cups flour (use GF mix & 2-1/4 tsp. Xanthan)

1-1/4 tsp. baking soda (GF add 1/2 tsp. baking powder)

1-1/2 tsp. salt

1. Cook over low heat: 1-1/2 cups brown sugar, 3/4 cup butter and 2 Tbs. water until melted.

2. Remove and Add: 1 (12-ounce) package semisweet chocolate chips; stir. Cool 10 minutes

3. Add: 2 eggs and beat well.

4. Add in the dry ingredients and mix well.

5. Chill for 1 hour and then drop onto a foil lined cookie sheet and bake at 350 degrees for 10 minutes. Do not overcook.

6. Immediately top each cookie with an Andes Mint (54) and when soft, spread on cookie.

RAISIN FILLING FOR RAISIN-FILLED SUGAR COOKIES

Grandma Smith - Use with dough recipe above for the raisin-filled cookies on page 175.

2 cups raisins

1 cup water

1/4 cup sugar

2 Tbs. butter

3/4 tsp. cinnamon

Dash salt

1/4 tsp. lemon juice

3 Tbs. cold water

2 Tbs. cornstarch

1. Bring raisins, water and salt to a boil. Add sugar, butter, cinnamon and lemon juice.

2. Dissolve cornstarch in water and add to mixture. Cook and stir until thickened. Cool.

LEMON THYME SHORTBREAD COOKIES

Yummy!

3/4 cup softened butter

1/2 cup powdered sugar

1 Tbs. grated lemon zest

2 tsp. dried thyme leaves (2 Tbs. fresh)

1/4 tsp. salt

1. In a medium bowl, beat butter and sugar until creamy. Add lemon zest and thyme; mix.

2. In a small bowl combine flour and salt; gradually add to the mixture.

3. Shape mixture into 2 (10-inch) logs; wrap in plastic wrap, and chill for 1 hour.

4. Preheat oven to 350 degrees. Line the baking sheets with parchment paper.

5. Unwrap dough and cut into 1/3 inch thick slices. Place on pans about 1 inch apart.

6. Bake for 11 minutes. Let cool on pans for 2 minutes. Remove; cool. Store in airtight container for up to I week.

NICHOLEEN'S NO-BAKE COOKIES OR ELEPHANT DROPS

1/2 cup butter

1/2 cup milk

1/4 cup cocoa, or to taste

2 cups sugar

Dash of salt

1 tsp. vanilla

4 cups quick oats (use GF)

1. In a large saucepan add 1/2 cup butter and melt it. Add 1/2 cup milk, 1/4 cup or less cocoa, and 2 cups sugar; stir and heat until boiling.

2. Bring to a rolling boil and then remove from heat. Add 1 tsp. vanilla, a dash of salt; then add 4 cups of quick oats (if using regular oats blend first to make smaller). Stir in until mixture is chocolate covered and not runny—add more oats if it is.

3. Immediately drop by teaspoons on waxed paper to cool for 5-10 minutes.

VARIATION:
 ✓ *May also add 1/3 cup peanut butter and lessen cocoa to taste, if desired.*

JANEEN'S SUGAR COOKIES

1 cup shortening

2 tsp. vanilla

2 cups sugar

2 eggs

4 cups flour (GF mix & 2 tsp. Xanthan)

4 tsp. baking powder

1/2 tsp. salt

1/4 cup milk

1. Cream: 1 cup shortening, 2 tsp. vanilla, and 2 cups sugar

2. Add: 2 eggs, one at a time and mix after each addition.

3. Add: 4 cups flour (GF mix & 2 tsp. Xanthan), 4 tsp. baking powder, 1/2 tsp. salt, and 1/4 cup milk. Mix until blended.

4. Chill for at least 1 hour and then roll out into desired shapes.

5. Bake at 375 degrees for 10 minutes. Cool.

BECKY'S CHOCOLATE BARS

Sugar Free and Dairy Free Chocolate Chips or Chocolate Bars!

1/4 cup cocoa powder

1/4 cup coconut oil, melted

3 Tbs. sweetener of choice-- agave, honey, pure maple syrup, or vanilla stevia drops

1/4 tsp. vanilla, optional

1. Combine coconut oil and agave, maple syrup or stevia (has aftertaste).

2. Stir in cocoa powder until it gets thick. If too thick, add 1 Tbs. oil.

3. Pour into any flat container. Freeze.

4. Either chop for chips or melt for chocolate sauce. Store this in the freezer in ziploc bags.

5. By adding craisins or nuts before freezing, these can be chocolate nut or fruit bars.

BECKY FISHER'S HEALTHY BANANA COOKIES

3 ripe bananas, mashed

2 cups rolled oats (use GF)

1 cup dates; pitted and chopped

1/3 cup vegetable oil or coconut oil

1 tsp. vanilla

Chocolate chips, if desired

1. Stir all together and let sit 15 minutes.

2. Drop by spoonfuls on ungreased cookie sheet. Bake at 350 degrees for 20 minutes.

KELSIE'S PROTEIN BITES

1 cup dry oatmeal (use Gluten Free)

1 cup coconut flakes (unsweetened)

1/2 cup chocolate chips (dark or semi-sweet)

1/2 cup peanut butter (I use all natural peanut butter)

1/2 cup flaxseed meal

1/3 cup honey (I melt mine in the microwave so it's easier to stir in)

1 tsp. vanilla

1/4 cup chia seeds (I use white, they also come in black)

1. Mix everything together and then spoon onto a cookie sheet with wax paper. I use my cookie scoop to scoop them onto the cookie sheet.

2. Let cookies sit in the fridge for 39 min and then transfer them into a storage container and keep in the fridge for up to 2 weeks.

GLUTEN FREE PALEO CHOCOLATE CHIP COOKIES

3 cups blanched Almond flour

1/2 cup virgin coconut oil, unrefined

1/2 cup pure Maple syrup

2 eggs

1 tsp. baking soda

1 tsp. salt

1 tsp. vanilla extract

1-1/2 cups semi-sweet chocolate chips

1. Preheat oven to 350 degrees.

2. In a medium sized mixing bowl combine dry ingredients.

3. In a small mixing bowl beat eggs, maple syrup, and vanilla extract with a hand mixer.

4. Pour wet ingredients into dry and beat with hand mixer until combined.

5. Melt coconut oil, pour into batter, and continue to blend until combined.

6. Stir in chocolate chips.

7. On a parchment lined baking sheet, drop balls of cookie dough, about a tablespoon in size. *This is a must --if you don't use parchment, they stick.*

8. Bake for 9 minutes let cool on baking sheet.

9. Let cool and serve with a cold glass of almond milk!

ALMOND COOKIES – GLUTEN FREE AND DAIRY FREE

1/4 cup coconut oil

1/4 cup coconut sugar

1/4 cup pure maple syrup

1-1/2 cups almond meal

1/4 -1/2 tsp. salt

1/2 tsp. baking soda

1/3 cup dark chocolate chips

1/2 tsp. coconut oil

Sliced almonds

1. Preheat oven to 375 degrees. Line a baking sheet with parchment paper.

2. Mix first 6 ingredients. Place on parchment and roll out to a 1/4-inch thickness. Bake 8 to 10 min.

3. Cool slightly and then score the cookies into 2" squares. Place an almond on each square. Cool.

4. In the microwave, melt the chocolate chips and coconut oil and then drizzle over the cookies.

COCONUT MACAROONS

1 (14 oz.) bag of coconut

1 can sweetened condensed milk

1 tsp. vanilla

Melted chocolate if desired

1. Preheat oven to 350 degrees.

2. Mix coconut, milk and vanilla. Scoop the cookies onto a well-greased cookie sheet.

3. Bake 10-15 minutes.

4. Cookies will be brown on bottom. Remove promptly from pan and cool.

5. Dip bottoms or 1/2 of each cookie in chocolate when cool and let set.

182

GLUTEN FREE SUGAR COOKIES

This can also be used for fruit cookie pizza or pie crust.

1-1/4 cup butter

3/4 cup instant vanilla pudding mix

1/2 cup sugar

2 eggs

2 tsp. vanilla

4 cups Featherlight mix - or regular flour for non-GF

2 tsp. xanthan gum - leave out for non-GF

3/4 tsp. baking powder

1/4 tsp. salt

1. Cream the butter, pudding mix and sugar. Add eggs one at a time, beating well after each. Add vanilla. Combine dry ingredients and add to creamed mixture. Chill 1 hour.

2. Preheat oven to 350 degrees. Sprinkle a surface with potato starch. Place dough on surface and turn once to coat.

3.   Roll or pat to 1/4 inch thick. Cut in shapes and place cookies 1-inch apart on baking sheets.

4. Bake 11 minutes. Frost

ANNETTE'S GLUTEN FREE SUGAR COOKIES

1 cup shortening (Don't use butter Crisco)

1 cup sugar

2 eggs

1/2 tsp. vanilla

2 cups rice flour

2/3 cup cornstarch (I use 1/3 potato starch and 1/3 cup cornstarch)

1/3 cup tapioca starch

2 tsp. xanthan gum

2 tsp. baking powder

1/2 tsp. soda

1/2 tsp. salt

3/4 cup sour cream

1. Cream the shortening and sugar. Add eggs and vanilla and combine.

2. Whisk the dry ingredients together. Mix the wet and dry ingredients. Add sour cream last. Chill dough for at least an hour. Roll out thick with powdered sugar instead of flour.

3. Can double or triple the recipe. Dough freezes well. Bake at 350 degrees for 8-10 min.

For Non-GF: Use 3 cups of regular flour and leave out the Xanthan

BAR COOKIES

SNACKIN' GRANOLA BARS

3-1/2 cups oats, toasted (use GF)

1 cup raisins

1/2 cup brown sugar

1/3 cup honey, corn syrup or molasses

1 egg

1/2 tsp. salt

2/3 cup melted butter

1/2 tsp. vanilla

1 cup chopped nuts

Chocolate chips if desired

1. Place 3-1/2 cups oats on a sided baking sheet. Toast oats at 350 degrees for 15 minutes.

2. Combine together: 1 cup raisins, 1/2 cup brown sugar, 1/3 cup honey, corn syrup or molasses, 1 egg, 1/2 tsp. salt, 2/3 cup melted butter, 1/2 tsp. vanilla, 1 cup chopped nuts, and chocolate chips is desired.

3. Add in the toasted oats and combine all ingredients. Press into a baking pan.

4. Bake at 350 degrees for 20 minutes. Cool, cut into bars.

RHUBARB CRUMB BARS

These bars can also be made with 1/2 rhubarb and 1/2 strawberries

Streusel:

6 Tbs. unsalted butter, melted

1 cup flour (use GF mix)

1/2 cup brown sugar

1/4 tsp. salt

Cake:

1/2 pound rhubarb, cut into 1/2-inch pieces (1 ½ cups)

1 Tbs. brown sugar

1 cup flour (GF mix & 1/2 tsp. Xanthan)

1/2 tsp. baking powder

1/4 tsp. salt

1/2 tsp. vanilla

1/2 cup unsalted room temperature butter

1 cup powdered sugar

2 large eggs

1. *Make the Streusel:* Mix until combined: 6 Tbs. unsalted butter, melted, 1 cup flour (GF mix), 1/2 cup brown sugar, and 1/4 tsp. salt; set aside.

2. Preheat oven to 350 degrees.

3. Butter an 8-9-inch square baking pan. Line the pan with parchment paper; leaving a 2-inch overhang on two sides. Butter and flour the parchment paper, tapping out excess flour.

4. *Make the cake:* In a medium bowl, combine rhubarb, brown sugar, and 1/4 cup flour (GF); set aside. In another bowl whisk all remaining dry ingredients together.

5. In a large bowl, beat butter and powdered sugar until light and fluffy; beat in eggs, one at a time and then mix in vanilla and the flour mixture.

6. Spread into prepared pan. Sprinkle with rhubarb and top with streusel.

7. Bake until golden and a toothpick inserted in center comes out with moist crumb attached—about 45-50 minutes. Let cool completely. Using paper overhang, lift cake from pan. Cut into 16 bars.

JANELLE'S TWIX BARS

Crust:

1-1/4 cups flour (GF mix & 2/3 tsp. Xanthan)

1/4 cup sugar

1/2 cup butter, room temperature

1/2 tsp. salt

Caramel:

1/2 cup butter

1/2 cup brown sugar

2 Tbs. corn syrup

1/2 cup sweetened condensed milk

1/2 tsp. vanilla

Dash of salt

Top Layer:

1-2 cups of chocolate chips

1 tsp. shortening

1. *Make the crust:* Combine 1-1/4 cups flour (GF mix & 2/3 tsp. Xanthan), 1/4 cup sugar, and 1/2 cup butter, room temperature. Crumble crust ingredients together. Pack into a 9x9 pan that has been sprayed, and lined with foil and then sprayed again. Bake at 350 degrees for 15 to 20 minutes.

2. *Make the caramel layer:* Combine 1/2 cup butter, 1/2 cup brown sugar, 2 Tbs. corn syrup, and 1/2 cup sweetened condensed milk in heavy saucepan. Bring to boil over medium heat. Boil 5 minutes, stirring constantly, as it burns easily. Remove from heat. Stir with a spoon slowly until it shows signs of thickening. Pour over crust and let cool a little.

3. *Make the top layer:* Melt approximately 1-2 cups of chocolate chips with 1 tsp. shortening over low heat or in the microwave. Pour over the caramel layer and spread carefully. Chill. Cut into bars.

4. This can be doubled and put it in a 9x13 pan.

HERSHEY'S 5-MINUTE BROWNIE RECIPE

3⁄4 cup Hershey's cocoa

2 cups sugar

1⁄2 tsp. baking soda

2 eggs

2⁄3 cup vegetable oil

1⁄2 cup boiling water (measure accurately)

1-1⁄3 cups flour (GF mix & 3⁄4 tsp. Xanthan)

1 tsp. vanilla

1⁄4 tsp. salt

1. Stir cocoa and baking soda in mixing bowl.

2. Blend in 1⁄3 cup oil.

3. Add boiling water; stir until mixture thickens.

4. Stir in sugar, eggs and remaining 1⁄3 cup oil; stir until smooth.

5. Add flour, vanilla and salt and blend completely.

6. Pour into lightly greased 9x13 pan or 2-8 x 8 pans.

7. Bake at 350 degrees for 35-40 minutes for 9 x 13 and 30-32 minutes for an 8 x 8 pan

8. Cool and frost if desired

MINT OR PEPPERMINT CANDY CANE BROWNIES

4 (1-ounce) squares unsweetened baking chocolate

1 cup butter

4 eggs

2 cups sugar

1 tsp. vanilla

1-1/4 cups flour (GF mix & 2/3 tsp. Xanthan)

1/2 tsp. baking powder

Frosting:

1-2 Tbs. milk

2 cups powdered sugar

1/4 cup butter, softened

1-1/2 tsp. peppermint extract (or flavor of your choice)

Green or pink food coloring

Chocolate Glaze:

6 ounces (1 cup) semisweet chocolate chips

6 Tbs. butter (unsalted)

1. Preheat the oven to 350 degree. Line a 9 x 13-inch pan with foil, making sure the foil extends over the edge by at least on inch. Lightly spray with nonstick cooking spray.

2. Chop both the unsweetened chocolate and the butter and place in a microwave-safe bowl. Microwave 30 seconds; stir. Repeat if necessary, until melted.

3. With an electric mixer, beat eggs, sugar, and vanilla for 2 minutes. Meanwhile, measure out flour and baking powder. With the mixer, slowly add the melted chocolate and butter; mix in. Slowly add in the flour mix and beat until just combined. Pour into prepared pan and bake for 20-30 minutes or until a knife poked in center comes out clean.

4. Cool completely on a metal rack. When brownies are cool, prepare frosting. Combine all frosting ingredients, starting with 1-1/2 Tbs. milk. Beat until light and fluffy. Add the milk slowly by one teaspoon at a time. Spread over the brownies. Chill in the refrigerator.

5. Prepare glaze while brownies are chilling, combine ingredients and microwave to melt, starting with 30-second intervals. Top the chilled brownies with glaze and return to the refrigerator to set. To serve, lift out by the foil and cut into squares.

VARIATION: For candy cane brownies use red food coloring to make pink frosting and 1/2 - 1 tsp. peppermint extract to flavor. Use 1/2-1 cup of crushed candy canes on top of the glaze.

BEST EVER BROWNIES OR GLUTEN FREE BROWNIES

Nicholeen Peck

1/2 cup butter

1/2 cup cocoa or 4 squares baking chocolate

2 cups sugar

4 eggs

1 tsp. vanilla

1-1/2 cups flour (GF use: 1/2 cup rice flour, 1/2 cup tapioca starch, 1/2 cup cornstarch, and 1 tsp. xanthan gum)

1/2 tsp. salt

Chopped nuts--optional

Icing:

3 cups powdered sugar

1/4 cup butter

1/4 cup cocoa

1 egg or 3 Tbs. water

3 Tbs. hot milk

Decorative colored sprinkles, if desired

1. Preheat oven to 350 degrees. Grease a 9 x 13 pan.

2. In a saucepan melt the 1/2 cup butter; then add 1/2 cup cocoa or 4 squares baking chocolate and melt together. Remove from heat and add 2 cups sugar. Add 4 eggs, stirring one in at a time, until blended. Add the 1 tsp. vanilla, 1/2 tsp. salt, and nuts-optional; mix in.

3. Add in the flour and blend all together. Pour into pan.

4. Bake 30 minutes---do not over bake. Let cool and then frost with the icing below.

5. Make the Icing while the cake is cooling slightly. Mix 3 cups powdered sugar, 1/4 cup butter, 1/4 cup cocoa, 1 egg or 3 Tbs. water, and 3 Tbs. hot milk until smooth.

6. Frost and decorate with sprinkles, if desired.

7. This recipe makes a 9 x 13 pan or a large baking sheet with sides if you *double* it.

MASTER MIX FOR BROWNIES

Master Mix: **Makes 12 (9x9) pans or 6 (9x13) pans**

6 cups flour (use a GF mix and 3 tsp. Xanthan gum)

8 cups sugar

2 Tbs. baking powder (GF use 3 Tbs.)

2 Tbs. salt

3 cups cocoa

2 cups shortening

1. Mix dry ingredients and cut in shortening.

2. Blend well.

3. Store mix in an airtight container at room temperature.

BROWNIES FROM MASTER MIX

For One 9x9 Pan or 8x8 Pan (Double this for a 9x13 pan)

2 cups Master Mix

2 eggs

1 tsp. vanilla

1/2 cup chopped nuts or chocolate chips, optional

1. Mix until blended.

2. Bake in a greased pan at 375 for 20 minutes for a 9 x 9 pan or 25 minutes for an 8x8 pan.

BLACK BOTTOM BROWNIES

Prepared mix above for a pan of brownies from the Master Mix or box mix

1 (8-oz.) pkg. cream cheese

1 large egg

1/2 cup sugar

1. Prepare a recipe for brownies above and put into the 8 x 8 square pan.

2. Beat 1 pkg. (8 oz.) cream cheese with 1 large egg and 1/2 cup sugar until smooth.

3. Spread over the brownie mix and bake at 350 degrees for 45 minutes or until a toothpick comes out clean.

FUDGIE SCOTCH SQUARES

1-1/2 cups graham cracker crumbs (use GF)

1 can Eagle Brand Sweetened Condensed Milk

1 cup butterscotch chips

1 cup semi-sweet chocolate chips

1 cup chopped walnuts or nuts of your choice

1. Mix all ingredients and press into a very well-greased 9 x 9 pan.

2. Bake at 350 degrees for 30-35 minutes. Cool 45 minutes and cut into 1-1/2 inch squares.

3. Makes 25

EVELYN'S BROWNIES

1 cup shortening or oil

3 (1 oz.) squares of baking chocolate; melted (or use 1/2 cup cocoa mixed with 3 Tbs. butter, melted)

2 cups sugar

1 cup flour (GF mix & 1/2 tsp. Xanthan)

4 eggs; beaten

1 cup of chopped nuts

1 tsp. vanilla

Dash of salt

1. Mix together: 1 cup shortening or oil and 3 squares of baking chocolate; melted (or use 1/2 cup cocoa mixed with 3 Tbs. butter, melted).

2. Mix in another bowl, mix: 2 cups sugar and 1 cup flour (GF mix & 1/2 tsp. Xanthan)

3. In yet another bowl mix: 4 eggs; beaten, 1 cup of chopped nuts, 1 tsp. vanilla and a dash of salt.

4. Combine all together, pour into a 9 x 13 baking dish and bake at 350 degrees for 30 minutes. These are fudgy brownies.

JUNE'S BEST CAKE BROWNIES

Pat Garrard

1/2 to 1 cup softened butter –I usually use only 1/2 cup

1 cup sugar

1 (16-ounce) can Hershey chocolate syrup

4 eggs

1 tsp. vanilla

1 cup flour (GF mix & 1/2 tsp. Xanthan)

1/2 tsp. salt

Glaze:

>**1 cup sugar**
>
>**1/3 cup butter**
>
>**1/3 cup milk**
>
>**2/3 cup semi-sweet chocolate chips**
>
>**2/3 cup of mini-marshmallows**

1. Cream butter, sugar. Add eggs 1 at a time; beating well after each addition. Mix in chocolate syrup and vanilla. Add flour and salt. Stir until well blended.

2. Pour into a greased 15x10 (a broiler pan or jelly roll) pan. Bake at 350 degrees for 20-25 minutes, or until toothpick still has crumbs on it.

3. *Make the Glaze*: Combine in a saucepan the butter and sugar, and milk. Bring to a boil until sugar is dissolved. Remove from the heat and stir in chocolate chips and marshmallows. Stir until melted. Pour over brownies and spread evenly. Cool and cut.

DEBBIE POND'S BLOND BROWNIES

>**1 cup flour (GF mix & 1/2 tsp. Xanthan)**
>
>**1/2 tsp. baking powder**
>
>**1/8 tsp. baking soda**
>
>**1/2 tsp. salt**
>
>**1/2 cup nuts**
>
>**1/3 cup butter**
>
>**1 cup brown sugar**
>
>**1 Tbs. vanilla**
>
>**1 egg**

1. Melt butter and mix in sugar. Cool. Add egg, vanilla and dry ingredients; blend well.

2. Bake at 350 degrees for 20-25 min. in a greased 8x8 pan. Double for a 9x13 pan and cook 30 minutes.

TANGY LEMON SQUARES

Crust:

1 cup butter, softened

1/2 cup powdered sugar

2 cups flour (GF mix & 1 tsp. Xanthan)

Filling:

2 cups sugar

1/3 cup lemon juice- bottled

1 tsp. baking powder

4 eggs

1/3 cup flour (GF mix)

Topping:

2 Tbs. powdered sugar

1. In a large bowl, cream together butter and the 1/2 cup powdered sugar until fluffy. Add 2 cups of the flour, beating until blended. Spread evenly over the bottom of a well-greased 9x13 pan. Bake in a 350 degree oven for 20 minutes.

2. Meanwhile, beat eggs until foamy and then add the sugar. Beat until thick and blended.

3. Add lemon juice, remaining 1/3 cup flour, and baking powder; beat until thoroughly blended. Pour lemon mixture over baked crust and return to oven.

4. Bake 25-30 minutes or until golden and custard is set. Remove from oven and sprinkle evenly with 2 Tbs. powdered sugar; let cool.

5. To serve, cut in small squares or bars. Makes about 20 pieces

GLUTEN FREE BANANA BARS

1/2 cup butter

1-1/2 cups sugar

2 eggs

3/4 cup sour cream

2 ripe bananas, mashed (1 cup)

1 tsp. vanilla

1-1/2 cups rice flour

1 tsp. soda

1/3 cup potato starch

1/4 cup tapioca starch

1 tsp. Xanthan

1/8 tsp. salt

1. In a large bowl, beat together butter and sugar. Add eggs, bananas, and vanilla; mix well.

2. In a medium bowl, combine the dry ingredients. Add to sugar mixture alternately with the sour cream. Mix well.

3. Spread into a greased and rice floured 17 x 11 x 1-inch jelly roll pan or 2-9 x 13 pans.

4. Bake at 350 degrees for 18 to 25 minutes or until mixture leaves sides of pan and tests done.

5. Cool and frost with sour cream frosting (recipe below). This freezes well without the frosting.

For Non-GF: Add 2-1/8 cups flour and no Xanthan, potato or tapioca starch and no rice flour.

SOUR CREAM FROSTING FOR THE BANANA BARS

1/4 cup shortening

1/4 cup butter

1/2 tsp. vanilla

1/4 cup sour cream

2 cups powdered sugar

1. In a medium mixing bowl, mix all ingredients and beat until smooth.

2. Frost

GLUTEN-FREE RHUBARB BARS

2 cups gluten-free all-purpose flour mix or regular flour for non-GF

1 tsp. baking powder

1/2 cup cold butter

2 eggs, beaten

3 Tbs. 2% milk

5 cups sliced fresh or frozen rhubarb, thawed

1 pkg. (3 oz.) strawberry gelatin

Topping:

1 cup sugar

1 cup gluten-free all-purpose flour mix or regular flour for non-GF

1/2 cup cold butter

1. In a large bowl, combine flour & baking powder. Cut in butter until mixture resembles coarse crumbs. Stir in eggs and milk just until moistened.

2. Press onto the bottom of a 15-in. x 10-in. x 1-in. baking pan coated with cooking spray.

3. Top with rhubarb and sprinkle with gelatin.

4. Make the topping: In a small bowl, combine sugar and flour. Cut in butter until mixture resembles coarse crumbs. Sprinkle over top.

5. Bake at5 375 for 35-40 minutes or until lightly browned. Cool on wire rack. Cut into bars. Yield: 3 dozen

PUMPKIN SPICE ENERGY BARS

Gluten-free and Dairy-free

2 cups gluten free oats (use regular oats if not GF)

1/2 teaspoon kosher salt

1 teaspoon ground cinnamon

1/4 teaspoon ground nutmeg

Pinch of cloves

2 eggs

1/2 teaspoon vanilla extract

1 cup almond milk

10 oz. pumpkin butter

2 tablespoons hemp seed

3 tablespoons unsweetened coconut

1/4 cup chopped pecans

1/4 cup mini dark chocolate chips

1. Preheat oven to 400F degrees.

2. In a large bowl, combine oats, salt, cinnamon, nutmeg and cloves.

3. In a medium bowl, combine eggs, vanilla, almond milk and pumpkin butter; mix thoroughly. Stir wet mixture into dry mixture mix thoroughly.

4. Stir in hemp seeds, coconut, pecans and chocolate chips; stir just to combine.

5. Press energy bar mixture into a greased 9" loaf pan. Bake in preheated oven for 45 minutes or until the edges start to brown and the center is set. Remove from oven and let cool on a baking rack for 15 minutes before removing from pan to cool completely.

6. When fully cool, slice into 12-14 bars. Wrap individually and store in fridge or freezer. This is important to help the bars set.

7. Take on a hike and enjoy! Yield: 12-14 bars

RICE KRISPIES MARSHMALLOW TREATS

1/4 cup butter

6-10 ounces regular marshmallows (about 40) or 4 cups mini marshmallows

5-6 cups Rice Krispies

1. Melt butter in 3-quart pan. Add marshmallows and cook over very low heat, stirring constantly, until marshmallows are melted and mixture is syrupy. Remove from heat.

2. Add Rice Krispies and stir until well coated.

3. Press warm mixture evenly and firmly in buttered 9x13 baking pan. Cut into squares when cool.

4. Yield: 24 squares; 2x2 inches

CANDY, CANDY

ALMOND NUT CLUSTERS

I make these every Christmas---it's a tradition!

2 cups whole raw almonds

1/2 cup sugar

1 tsp. vanilla

2 Tbs. unsalted butter

3/4 tsp. salt

1. Heat almonds, sugar, and butter in a 9-inch skillet over medium heat, stirring constantly until golden, about 15 minutes.

2. Remove from heat; stir in vanilla. Spread mixture on buttered foil or baking sheet.

3. Sprinkle with salt. Cool completely. Break into clusters.

CANDIED WALNUTS OR PECANS

1 cup brown sugar

1 cup sugar

1 cup sour cream

1-1/2 pounds walnuts or pecans

1. Cook the above in a heavy saucepan until the medium hard-ball stage (245 degrees)

2. Pour in 1-1/2 pounds walnuts or pecans.

3. Pour out on buttered foil. Cool and break into clusters.

ALMOND BARK (WHITE CHOCOLATE) POPCORN

1 package almond bark or white chocolate

3-4 quarts or so of popped popcorn

1. Melt Almond bark in microwave 1 min. 30 seconds. Stir, then microwave 30 more seconds. Pour over popped popcorn and mix.

2. Pour out on buttered foil and let cool. Break into clusters. Enjoy!

3. This recipe isn't precise. I just melt and pour until desired amount of almond bark is on the popcorn. Some people like it all covered and some just a bit. Find your mix!

OVEN CARAMEL CORN – LIKE CRACKER JACK

2 cups brown sugar

2 sticks butter (1 cup)

1/2 cup white corn syrup

6 quarts popped popcorn

1 tsp. salt

1 tsp. baking soda

1 tsp. butter flavoring

Nuts, if desired

1. Boil brown sugar, butter, syrup, and salt for 5 minutes.

2. Add baking soda and butter flavoring and pour over popped popcorn. Mix well.

3. Spread on cookie sheets. Place in a 200 degree oven for 1 hour, stirring every 15 minutes.

4. Remove from oven and let cool. Store it in a covered container to keep crisp.

CHOCOLATE CREAM CHEESE BALLS

Gayle Fryer

2 large (8 ounce) plain Hershey Bars or Symphony Bars

8 ounces Cool Whip

8 ounces cream cheese, room temperature

Chopped walnuts, crushed vanilla wafers (GF) or whatever sounds good to you

1. Break up bars and melt slowly in the microwave, stirring about every 30 seconds or more often. Let stand 2-3 minutes to cool.

2. Add softened cream cheese and stir well, and then let stand 4 minutes to cool.

3. Slowly add cool whip and mix well. Set in the refrigerator and let it cool.

4. When set, drop by teaspoons in chopped walnuts or crushed vanilla wafers and roll to coat.

5. Store in the refrigerator on a saran wrapped tray or platter. If storing for more than a few days, store in a covered container in the refrigerator.

202

GRANDMA (MARY) GUNDRY'S CARAMELS

1 can of Eagle Brand sweetened condensed milk (14 ounces)

3/4 pound butter - 1-1/2 cups

1 empty can filled with white sugar

1 empty can filled with brown sugar

1 empty can filled with white corn syrup

1. In a double boiler pan, place the condensed milk and the butter.

2. Fill the empty condensed milk can with: 1 can white sugar, 1 can brown sugar, and 1 can white corn syrup and add to double boiler.

3. In a double boiler, dissolve all ingredients and cook until medium firm ball – 250 degrees

4. Pour into lightly buttered dish; cool, cut and wrap in waxed paper squares. I love these plain, in turtles or whatever!

PEPPERMINT CHOCOLATE BRITTLE

1 bag white chocolate chips

1 bag semi-sweet chocolate chips

30 round peppermint candies or use candy canes; crushed

1. Line a 12 x 15 inch pan with foil.

2. Microwave the dark chocolate for 1-2 minutes until melted. Pour into foiled pan. Put in refrigerator to set.

3. Microwave white chocolate chips for 1-2 minutes until melted. Mix in crushed peppermint candies. Pour on top of semi-sweet chocolate.

4. Chill until set; about 1 hour. Break into pieces by slamming pan on the counter. Store the brittle in an airtight container.

MOTHER'S (BERNICE GUNDRY'S) CARAMELS AND TURTLES

2 cups white sugar

2 cups white corn syrup

2 cups whipping cream

1/2 tsp. salt

3/4 cup evaporated canned milk

6 Tbs. butter

1/2 Tbs. vanilla

1. Mix together in a heavy pan, the 2 cups white sugar, 2 cups white corn syrup, 2 cups whipping cream, and 1/2 tsp. salt. Stir until boiling on higher heat.

2. Gradually add 3/4 cup of evaporated milk and 6 Tbs. butter. Keep boiling until dissolved. Lower heat and stir occasionally until it reaches the firm soft ball stage or 250 degrees. Test a few drops in cold water to see if it forms a firm soft ball---firm enough to hold together well.

3. Add: 1/2 Tbs. vanilla. Stir and then cool down for 10 minutes off the heat.

4. Pour mixture into a buttered square pan and let it cool. These can be cut into (about 75) squares; and wrapped in wax paper or plastic wrap individually.

5. For Turtles: Place 3 individual pecan halves on a baking sheet. Place 1 tablespoon warm caramel from the pan over each pecan half and cool in a cool fruit room or in a cool garage until set. Dip into melted dipping chocolate and then set to cool again. If the caramel has already been poured into a buttered pan and cooled, cut into small squares and place one square on top of each pecan half and then dip in melted dipping chocolate and set to cool.

CINNAMON ROASTED ALMONDS

1 egg white

1 tsp. cold water

1 tsp. vanilla

1/4 tsp. salt

4 cups whole raw almonds

1/2 cup brown sugar

2 tsp. ground cinnamon

1. Preheat oven to 250 degrees. Put foil on a 10 x 15 jellyroll pan.

2. Lightly beat egg white; add water and beat until frothy but not stiff. Add nuts and stir well.

3. Mix together in another bowl the vanilla, sugar, salt, and cinnamon. Sprinkle over the nuts and toss to coat. Spread evenly onto pan.

4. Bake 1 hour, stirring occasionally until golden. Allow nuts to cool; store in a covered container.

CARNATION 5-MINUTE FUDGE

1-1/2 cups sugar

1-1/2 cups semi-sweet chocolate chips

1 tsp. vanilla

2 Tbs. butter

1/4 tsp. salt

2 cups mini marshmallows

1/2 chopped pecans or walnuts

2/3 cup evaporated milk

1. Line an 8-inch square pan with foil.

2. Combine sugar, milk, butter and salt in a medium, heavy-duty saucepan. Bring to full rolling boil over medium heat. Boil while stirring constantly, for 4 to 5 minutes.

3. Remove from heat. Stir in marshmallows, chips, nuts, and vanilla. Stir vigorously to melt the chips and marshmallows for about 1 minute.

4. Pour into pan and refrigerate for 2 hours.

5. To serve: Lift from pan; remove foil and cut into squares. Enjoy!

CARMALLOW POPCORN OR CORN CHEX

1/2 cup butter

1/2 cup brown sugar

3 cups mini marshmallows

2 quarts popcorn or corn Chex

Nuts, if desired

1. Place butter and sugar in glass dish and microwave for 2 minutes.

2. Stir and add 1 cup marshmallows. Microwave 1 minute more. Stir in an additional 2 cups of mini marshmallows and nuts if desired and pour over the popcorn and mix.

3. Pour out in a buttered 9 x 13 pan for bars or onto a buttered sheet pan to break into clusters. You can also make popcorn balls out of it, too. (I like it with Chex in clusters) Yield 8-10 balls

FESTIVE FUDGE WITH 4 VARIATIONS

Why Buy Fudge? This Makes About 2 Lbs. of Fudge!

3 cups (18 ounces) semi sweet or milk chocolate chips

1 (14-ounce) can Eagle Brand Sweetened Condensed Milk

Dash salt

1-1/2 tsp. vanilla

1. In a heavy saucepan, over low heat, melt chips with Eagle Brand milk and salt. Remove from heat; stir in nuts if desired and vanilla. Spread evenly into wax paper lined 8- or 9-inch square pan.

2. Chill 2 hours or until firm. Turn fudge onto cutting board, peel off paper, and cut into squares. Store covered in refrigerator.

VARIATIONS:

✓ *Chocolate Peanut Butter or Mint Chip Glazed Fudge: Proceed as above, stir in 3/4 cup peanut butter chips in place of nuts. Glaze: Melt 1/2 cup Peanut Butter or Mint Chips with 1/2 cup whipping cream; stir until thick and smooth. Spread over fudge.*

✓ *Marshmallow Fudge: Proceed as above, omit nuts and add 2 Tbs. butter to mixture; fold in 2 cups mini marshmallows.*

✓ *For Rocky Road: Proceed as above only add the nuts of your choice, too.*

✓ *Candy Cane Fudge: Proceed as above; omit nuts and add chopped candy canes and stir in.*

✓ *Gift Giving Tips: Create homemade gifts by serving up several varieties of fudge in decorative tins or boxes. Simply wrap up individual pieces in colored cellophane, candy wrappers, or candy cups and arrange in gift boxes or bags.*

SUCKERS WITH THREE VARIATIONS

Makes about 25

2 cups sugar

2/3 cup white corn syrup

1 cup water

Desired color

1 tsp. desired flavoring

1. In a heavy saucepan cook sugar, syrup, color, and water until it reaches 300 degrees.

2. Add 1 tsp. flavoring and immediately pour out into prepared and oiled sucker molds.

3. Cool and unmold.

VARIATIONS:
- ✓ *Butterscotch:* Add 1/2 cup butter and 1/4 tsp. salt after it boils
- ✓ *Peanut Butter:* Add 1/2 cup Peanut Butter after it reaches 300 degrees
- ✓ *Tootsie Pops:* Roll a small ball of tootsie roll onto the sucker stick (recipe below) and place in mold. Pour sucker mix on top.

TOOTSIE ROLLS

3 Tbs. butter

2 (1 ounce) squares of unsweetened baking chocolate

1/2 cup white corn syrup

1 tsp. vanilla

3/4 cup powdered milk

3 cups powdered sugar

1. Melt butter and chocolate. Add corn syrup and vanilla and heat.

2. Sift powdered milk and sugar until it is not grainy and then add.

3. Mix well; knead until smooth. Roll into logs or ball for suckers. Cut and wrap, if desired.

REESE'S PEANUT BUTTER BALLS / CUPS

1 cube butter-room temp

1 cup peanut butter

1/4 cup corn syrup

2 cup powdered sugar

dipping chocolate

1. Mix the above well and roll into the size balls that will fit into small candy cup wrapper.

2. Melt some dipping chocolate and place in the bottom of the candy cup; place Peanut Butter ball on top, and then pour more chocolate on top.

3. Freeze for 5 minutes to set and then store at room temperature.

CHOCOLATE PEPPERMINT MUDDY BUDDIES

8 cups Rice Chex Cereal

1 cup Mint Chocolate Chips

1/2 cup creamy peanut butter

1/4 cup butter (4 tablespoons)

1 teaspoon peppermint extract, or peppermint oil to taste

16 standard sized candy canes, divided (I like Bob's or Brach's)

1 cup powdered sugar

1. Place cereal in a large mixing bowl and set aside. Place 1 cup powdered sugar, and 8 candy canes in a food processor. Pulse several times to break up candy canes and then process until smooth. You'll have very tiny bits of candy cane still visible.

2. Place remaining 8 candy canes in a ziploc bag and use a heavy rolling pin, or meat mallet, or whatever the heck you want, to crush them into little bits. Set aside.

3. Place chocolate chips in a microwave safe bowl with peanut butter and butter. Heat chips in 30 second intervals, stirring in between, until melted and smooth. Stir in extract (or oil) and immediately pour over Chex mix.

4. Quickly pour in the crushed candy canes from the ziploc bag over the chocolate and then stir to coat the cereal. The chocolate mixture might be slightly thick, but keep stirring and it will coat everything.

5. Once the cereal mixture is coated with chocolate, dump in the powdered sugar mix and stir until everything is dusted in white.

CHOCOLATE MINT CHEX MIX

3 cups Chocolate Chex cereal

3 cups Corn Chex cereal

1/2 cup mint chocolate chips

1/2 cup peppermint flavored dark chocolate M&M's chocolate pieces

1. In a large microwaveable bowl, combine cereals; set aside. Line a sided cookie sheet with waxed paper or parchment paper.

2. In a medium microwaveable bowl, melt the mint chips on Medium (50%) about 1 minute; stir. Microwave another 15 seconds; stir. Repeat until chocolate is mostly melted and can be stirred smooth. Pour over cereal and evenly coat it.

3. Microwave uncovered on High for 3 minutes, stirring every minute. Spread on waxed paper and cool for 5 minutes. Stir in M&M's candies. Store covered.

VANILLA CHEX MIX

1 bag semi-sweet chocolate chips – chilled in freezer.

3 cups Corn Chex

3 cups Rice Chex

3 cups Wheat Chex (GF use more Rice or Corn Chex)

2 cups salted dry-roasted nuts

2 cups pretzel twists (use GF)

2 cups mini marshmallows

1 20-ounce Vanilla bark

1. Mix cereals, nuts, pretzels, marshmallows in a large bowl.

2. Melt Vanilla bark in microwave 1 min. 30 seconds. Stir, then microwave 30 more seconds. Stir, until smooth. Pour over cereal mix; add chocolate chips, stir.

3. Spread & cool on wax paper. Store this in an airtight container in the refrigerator.

210

CHEWY CHEX MIX

9 cups Rice Chex cereal

9 cups Corn Chex cereal

7 cups Golden Grahams cereal (GF--use Cinnamon Chex or Honey Nut Chex)

1 cup coconut

1/2 cup almonds

2 cups light Karo syrup

2 cups sugar

1-1/2 cups butter

1. Mix first 5 ingredients in a large bowl that has been lightly greased and set aside.

2. Bring remaining ingredients to a boil on the stove. Boil for 4 minutes while stirring constantly. Remove from heat and wait until boiling subsides; pour over the cereal mixture. Stir until cereal is covered. Spread mixture on cookie sheets or wax paper to cool. You may separate mixture into small portions or in one big bowl for everyone to share!

SUGARED CORN POPS

1 20-oz. bag corn pops (on the chip aisle usually)

2 cups sugar

1 Tbs. corn syrup

1/2 cup water

1 pound butter

1. Cook last 4 ingredients to soft crack stage; pour over the corn pops.

2. Mix and spread out to dry on a baking sheet. Break into clusters.

GOURMET CARAMEL/CHOCOLATE DIPPED PREZTAL RODS

Use The Information And Ingredients Listed Above In The Gourmet Caramel Apples For Pretzel Rods.

Large pretzel rods

Caramel, melted

Chocolate, melted

Sprinkles or toppings of choice

1. Cut large pretzel rods in half. Dip in melted caramel covering about 2/3 to 3/4 of pretzel. (Melt caramel as directed in recipe on page 212.)

2. Shake off excess caramel and place on a parchment paper covered tray and place in refrigerator to set. When set, dip in melted white or dark chocolate. (Melt chocolate as directed in recipe on page 212-213.) Return to refrigerator to set.

3. To decorate: drizzle with melted white or dark chocolate and return to refrigerator.

4. If you want to decorate with sprinkles or other toppings, immediately pour on them on while chocolate is still melted so they will stick. Put in the refrigerator to set.

5. When completely set, put in cellophane bags and tie with ribbon or raffia.

More instructions on page 212-213.

SCOTCHEROOS

This is a Pond family favorite!

1 cup sugar

1 cup white corn syrup

1 cup peanut butter (or Nutella)

6-7 cups Rice Krispies

1 cup semi-sweet chips

1 cup butterscotch chips

1. Melt sugar and syrup, but do not boil. Remove from heat and add Krispies and mix.

2. Pour into a 9 x 13 pan. Pat down with wet hands.

3. Melt chips and spread on the top. Cool and cut into squares.

NOTE:
✓ *If you use Nutella, the chocolate/butterscotch chip topping is optional.*

GOURMET CARAMEL APPLES

I Love These!

Apples: Any tart apple like Granny Smith, Jonathan Gold…Buy these in uniform size (Costco)

Sticks: Wooden sticks with a sharpened end work really well or a really thick sucker or a wooden Popsicle stick

Caramel: Peter's caramel is a commercial brand that comes in 5-lb. blocks and works well. (can order at gygi.com) One can also make your own.

White chocolate: Use Vanilla A'Peels

Chocolate: Use either milk or dark Chocolate A'Peels depending on your taste

Toppings: Use anything you want--crushed Oreo's, cinnamon sugar (a favorite), chopped nuts (peanuts, almonds, cashews, etc.), mini chocolate chips, mini m&m's, Heath toffee bits, crushed Butterfingers, chopped Snicker bars, sprinkles, crushed candy canes, or you can just layer and swirl the chocolate.

Size C4 Cellophane bags and ribbon for gift wrap

Parchment paper

Buy these and the other supplies at www.gygi.com

1. Wash, stem and dry COLD apples. Insert a stick and place on parchment paper on a baking sheet. Keep apples cold.

2. Melt caramel one of the 3 following ways:

   - *Microwave Method (I use this one): Cut caramel block in chunks and put into a microwave-safe dish. Cook on high for 1 minute. Stir. Using 50% power, cook for 1 minute. Stir again. Repeat at 50% power until thoroughly melted, being careful to not scorch caramel.*

   - *Double-boiler Method: Cut chunks of caramel and place in the top of a double boiler. Bring water to a simmer (do not boil) and stir until melted. Watch and stir; being careful to not scorch caramel. Turn heat down is needed.*

   - *Crock-pot Method: For a 5-lb block of caramel, heat chunks on high for 1-1/2 to 2 hours. Add also 5 capfuls of milk (use cap from a gallon of milk). Stir often. Use 1 capful of milk for each pound of caramel. Turn to low after.*

6. Dip cold apples in caramel and scrape excess caramel from the bottom of apple so you don't get a huge puddle of caramel on parchment. Use a big spoon to scrape and swirl off the excess. Place on the parchment paper covered tray. Put it in the refrigerator until caramel is set, about 15 minutes. (If it is cold when doing these, you can put them in a garage or outside.)

7. If you want nuts on the caramel, dip them in nuts right after dipping in caramel and before cooling. Set on tray after and cool.

8. For the next layer on top of the caramel, melt white or dark chocolate in deep microwave-safe dish by heating for 1 minute at 50% power (no higher or the chocolate will scorch). Stir and repeat at 30 second intervals (50% power); until chocolate is melted but still has a few small chunks left in it. Stir until completely melted. At this point your chocolate will be at the correct temperature for dipping. Dip caramel apples in chocolate of your choice. Scrape bottoms and place on tray and put in refrigerator to set.

9. *For Cinnamon-sugar apples*---tastes like apple pie--sprinkle cinnamon sugar over the apple right after you have dipped it into the white chocolate. Hold up-side down for a minute and then place on tray and put back in refrigerator.

10. For *apples with toppings*: After dipping in chocolate of choice, roll bottom 1/3 of apple in topping of your choice--Oreos, etc. Put on tray and back into the refrigerator to set.

11. *To make the chocolate drips* and drip patterns over the chocolate caramel apple, melt some white or dark chocolate in a ziploc bag; cut off a tiny corner and drizzle away!

12. *Store* any leftover caramel or chocolate in the container it was melted in in the cupboard to melt again and be able to make an apple fast for a spontaneous gift, etc.

13. When completely set, place in *cellophane bag* (will keep apple longer) and store in refrigerator. Tie bags with ribbon or raffia. Before eating, leave out on the counter for at least an hour so caramel is not rock hard and chocolate will not break off.

A FEW IDEAS:
- ✓ *Caramel, white chocolate and chocolate and white drizzles*
- ✓ *Caramel and nuts on the bottom;*
- ✓ *Caramel, chocolate, and sprinkles;*
- ✓ *Caramel and butterfingers;*
- ✓ *Caramel, white chocolate, cinnamon (2/3 sugar to 1/3 cinnamon) sugar (apple pie);*
- ✓ *Caramel, white chocolate, candy canes and chocolate chips and red/green sugar optional;*
- ✓ *Caramel, white chocolate or regular chocolate and Oreos, m & m's, snickers, etc.*
- ✓ *Just use your imagination!*

JUST DESSERTS

CHOCOLATE LAYER DESSERT –OR STRIPED DELIGHT!

1 cup flour (or GF flour mix)

1/2 cup butter

1 cup nuts

1 small pkg. instant chocolate pudding (use Pistachio for St. Patrick's Day)

1 small pkg. instant vanilla pudding

1 pkg. (8 ounce) cream cheese

3 cups milk

1 cup powdered sugar

1 (12-oz.) frozen whipped topping-Cool Whip

1. Mix the flour, butter and nuts together and pat into the bottom of a 13 x 9 baking dish.

2. Bake at 350 degrees for 10 minutes and let it cool. Meanwhile, beat the cream cheese, powdered sugar, and half of whipped topping together and spread over the cooled crust.

3. Combine puddings and milk; mix. Spread over the cream cheese mixture.

4. Top the layers with other half of whipped topping and a sprinkle of nuts. Keep covered and refrigerated. Serves 6-8

APPLE CRISP

8 cups sliced apples

2 tsp. cinnamon

2 cups sugar (1 cup brown and 1 cup white, if desired)

1 tsp. cinnamon

1-1/2 cups flour (or GF mix and 3/4 tsp. xanthan gum)

2/3 cup butter

Ice Cream or Whipped Cream for serving

1. Butter a 9 x 13-inch baking pan. Add 8 cups sliced apples and sprinkle with 2 tsp. cinnamon.

2. Sift together: 2 cups sugar (1 cup brown and 1 cup white), 1 tsp. cinnamon, and 1-1/2 cups flour (or GF mix and 3/4 tsp. xanthan gum).

3. Cut 2/3 cup butter into mixture until crumbly.

4. Place on top of the apples. Bake at 350 degrees for 45 minutes. Serve with ice cream or cream.

BERNICE GUNDRY'S PEACH STRUDEL DESSERT

1 to 2 quarts of canned peaches or sliced fresh peaches

1/2 cup shortening or butter

3/4 cup sugar

1-1/2 cups flour (use GF flour mix and 2/3 tsp. Xanthan)

3 tsp. baking powder

1/2 cup milk

1 Tbs. melted butter

1/4 cup brown sugar

1/2 cup chopped nuts

Whipped cream or ice cream to serve with

1. Put layers of canned peaches or sliced fresh peaches in the bottom of a 9 x 13 baking pan.

2. Mix together: 1/2 cup shortening, 3/4 cup sugar, 1-1/2 cups flour (GF flour mix and 2/3 tsp. Xanthan), 3 tsp. baking powder, and 1/2 cup milk. Spoon this over the peaches.

3. Mix 1 Tbs. melted butter, 1/4 cup brown sugar and 1/2 cup chopped nuts; sprinkle on top.

4. Bake at 350 degrees until done. Serve warm with whipped cream or ice cream.

APPLE DESSERT

6 large apples--sliced and put into an 8 x 8 buttered pan.

1 cup sugar

1 cup flour (GF mix and 1/2 tsp. xanthan gum)

1/2 tsp. salt

1 tsp. cinnamon

1 tsp. baking powder

1 egg

1/2 cup butter, melted

1. Place 6 large sliced apples into an 8 x 8 buttered pan.

2. Mix: 1 cup sugar, 1 cup flour (GF mix and 1/2 tsp. xanthan gum), 1/2 tsp. salt, 1 tsp. cinnamon, and 1 tsp. baking powder (1-1/2 tsp. for GF).

3. Add in 1 egg and mix. Spread over the apples. Melt 1/2 cup butter and pour over all.

4. Bake 350 for 25-35 minutes.

PEACH UPSIDE-DOWN CAKE

7 Tbs. room temperature unsalted butter

1/4 cup plus another 2/3 cup packed brown sugar

2 cups frozen sliced peaches, thawed and patted dry

1-1/4 cups flour (use Featherlight GF mix and add 1/2 tsp. xanthan gum)

1 tsp. baking powder

1/2 tsp. baking soda

1 tsp. cinnamon

Pinch of salt

1 large egg

1 tsp. vanilla

3/4 cup buttermilk

1. Preheat oven to 350 degrees. Melt 3 Tbs. butter in a small pan over low. Sprinkle in 1/4 cup brown sugar; stir until smooth. Spread in a 9-inch round cake pan. Arrange peaches on top in a single layer.

2. In a bowl, whisk flour, baking powder, soda, cinnamon, and salt. In another bowl, cream 4 Tbs. butter and 2/3 cup brown sugar until light and creamy, about 3 minutes.

3. Beat in egg and vanilla. Scrape down the bowl. Add 1/3 of the flour and mix until just combined. Mix in 1/2 of the buttermilk and 1/3 of the flour. Repeat with remaining buttermilk and flour.

4. Spread batter gently over peaches. Bake until a toothpick comes out clean, 35 to 40 minutes. Let cool for 5 minutes and then invert onto a plate.

BLACKBERRY PEACH CRISP

1 cup peeled peaches (2 medium)

3/4 cup blackberries

1 Tbs. flour (use GF)

1 Tbs. sugar

Couple dashes ground cinnamon and ground ginger

Topping:

3 Tbs. flour (use GF)

2 Tbs. sugar

2 Tbs. brown sugar

4 Tbs. chopped pecans

1/8 tsp. cinnamon

2 Tbs. cold butter

Serving:

Whipped cream or Vanilla Ice Cream

1. Preheat oven to 375 degrees. Line a small baking sheet with foil and set aside.

2. Combine peaches and blackberries in a bowl. Add flour, sugar, cinnamon, and ginger and toss to combine. Divide fruit between 2 ramekins or other small baking dishes (I used 4 small ramekins).

3. In a separate bowl, combine flour, sugar, brown sugar, nuts, and cinnamon. Add butter and use clean hands to break up pieces in flour mixture until it resembles coarse crumbs with a few larger pebble size pieces. Divide between ramekins.

4. Bake 30 to 35 minutes or until the topping is brown and crisp. Cool for at least 10 minutes before serving with cream or vanilla ice cream. Serves 2-4

CREAM CHEESE CUPCAKES

3 (8-oz.) pkgs. cream cheese

1-1/2 cups sugar, divided

5 eggs

1-3/4 tsp. vanilla, divided

1 cup sour cream

2 Tbs. jam; divided

1. Preheat oven to 325 degrees. Line 24 muffin tins with paper liners.

2. Beat cream cheese with 1 cup sugar and eggs. Add 1-1/2 tsp. vanilla.

3. Pour batter into muffin liners; filling 2/3 full. Bake 40 min.

4. To prepare filling: Mix sour cream, 1/4 cup sugar, and 1/4 tsp. vanilla.

5. Remove cupcakes from oven. They will fall in the middle. Fill the hole with the sour cream mixture. Spoon 1/4 tsp. of jam on top.

6. Return to oven and bake 5 minutes. Garnish with fresh berries.

FAVORITE FRUIT CRUNCH

5 cups fresh peaches, apples, rhubarb, etc.

1/2 cup sugar

1 tsp. cinnamon

1/2 tsp. nutmeg

Crumb Topping:

1 cup flour (GF mix or 2/3 cup rice flour, 1/4 cup potato starch, 2 Tbs. tapioca starch and 1/2 tsp. Xanthan)

1-1/2 tsp. baking powder

1/8 tsp. salt

1/2 cup brown sugar or white sugar

1 egg, beaten

1/2 cup butter

1/2 cup nuts, chopped, if desired

Ice cream or whipped topping to serve with; optional

1. Slice peaches or fruit of choice and place in bottom of a 2 quart baking dish (9 x 9). Mix 1/2 cup sugar, cinnamon, and nutmeg; sprinkle over the fruit.

2. *Make Crumb Topping:* In a medium bowl, combine flour, baking powder, salt, and sugar. Add egg and beat with hand mixer until crumbly. Sprinkle over the fruit.

3. Melt butter and drizzle over top of crumb mixture. Sprinkle with 1/2 cup chopped nuts, if desired.

4. Bake at 350 degrees for 40 to 45 minutes or until lightly browned and fruit tests done.

5. Serve with ice cream or whipped topping.

ALMOND TORTE

Gluten free and dairy free

Tip: Cut the paper liner before making the batter, but do not spray and line the pan until the batter is ready; this will prevent the spray from pooling in the bottom of the pan.

1-3/4 cups sliced blanched almonds

3/4 cup plus 2 tablespoons confectioners' or powdered sugar

4 large egg whites

1/4 teaspoon salt

1/2 teaspoon almond extract

Whipped cream, for serving (optional)

1. Preheat oven to 325 degrees. Cut a piece of wax or parchment paper to fit the bottom of an 8-inch round cake pan. Coat the pan with nonstick spray, place prepared paper round in bottom of pan, and spray paper. Sprinkle evenly with 1/4 cup almonds.

2. In a food processor, process remaining 1-1/2 cups almonds with 3/4 cup confectioners' sugar until finely ground; set aside.

3. In the bowl of an electric mixer fitted with the whisk attachment, beat egg whites with salt until soft peaks form. Gradually add remaining 2 tablespoons of confectioners' sugar and beat until stiff glossy peaks form. Beat in almond extract. In three additions, gently fold in ground almond mixture.

4. Evenly spread batter into prepared pan, tapping pan on counter to expel large air bubbles. Bake until golden brown and firm in center, 40 to 45 minutes; cool completely in pan. Invert onto serving plate, and remove wax or parchment paper.

COOK'S NOTE:
- ✓ *Grinding the almonds with the sugar keeps the mixture from getting oily and prevents a paste from forming.*

OLD FASHIONED RICE-CUSTARD PUDDING

3/4 cup minute rice or 1/2 cup regular rice

3 cups evaporated milk (2 large cans)

1 cup water

1/2 cup sugar

2 tsp. vanilla

2 eggs

1 cup raisins

Cinnamon and nutmeg, to taste

Butter

1. Cook rice as directed on package.

2. While cooking, whip 2 eggs. Add evaporated milk, water, sugar and vanilla.

3. Add cooked rice and 1 cup raisins.   Pour into a baking dish.

4. Sprinkle with nutmeg and cinnamon until top is covered. Dot the top with butter.

5. Bake at 375 degrees until mixture begins to bubble (about 1/2 hour). Do not boil. Allow to cool slightly before serving.

224

RICE PUDDING

1 cup of rice

2-1/2 cups water

1 tsp. salt

2 eggs

2 cups whole milk or half and half

3/4 cup sugar

1 tsp. vanilla

1/2 cup raisins

Dash of nutmeg

Cinnamon

1. Cook 1 cup of rice in 2-1/2 cups water with 1 tsp. salt until rice is tender and water is absorbed.

2. Beat 2 eggs; add 2 cups whole milk or half and half, 3/4 cup sugar, 1 tsp. vanilla, 1/2 cup raisins and a dash of nutmeg.

3. Pour into a baking dish and sprinkle top with cinnamon. Bake at 325 degrees until set.

JANEEN'S EASY RICE PUDDING

3 cups of cold cooked rice

2 cups half and half (or evaporated milk, regular milk or sweetened condensed milk and milk mixed to make 2 cups)

2 eggs beaten

1/2 cube butter (4 Tbs)

1/2 cup to 1 cup sugar, to taste

Dash of salt

1-2 tsp. vanilla

Cinnamon; to taste or use about 1/8 tsp. to 1/4 tsp

Nutmeg; to taste or use about 1/8 tsp. to 1/4 tsp

1. Beat the 2 eggs into the 2 cups of milk of choice above.

2. Combine all ingredients above into a saucepan when they are cold or room temperature so your eggs don't cook too fast. Stir constantly on just above medium heat until thickens.

3. Remove from heat and add 1-2 tsp. vanilla depending on vanilla strength. Add cinnamon and nutmeg to taste. Eat and enjoy! This can be eaten cold or warm.

INDIVIDUAL CHEESE CAKES

2 (8 ounce) pkgs. softened cream cheese

2 eggs

3/4 cup sugar

1 tsp. lemon juice

18 vanilla wafer cookies (use GF)

Cherry pie filling or your favorite flavor

1. Beat until fluffy: 2 (8 ounce) pkgs. softened cream cheese, 2 eggs, 3/4 cup sugar, and 1 tsp. lemon juice

2. Place a Vanilla Wafer or a Gluten Free cookie in the bottom of a cupcake paper that has been placed in a muffin tin (approx. 18).

3. Spoon 1 Tablespoon to 1-1/2 Tbs. of the cream cheese mixture on top of the cookie.

4. Bake 15-20 minutes at 350 degrees. Cool, peel off paper and top with a teaspoon of cherry pie filling.

NEW YORK STYLE CHEESECAKE

1-1/2 cups graham cracker crumbs (use GF)

3 Tbs. sugar

1/3 cup butter, melted

4 (8 oz.) pkgs. cream cheese, softened

1 cup sugar

1 tsp. vanilla

4 eggs

1. Mix graham cracker crumbs, 3 Tbs. sugar and butter; press onto the bottom of a 9-inch springform pan.

2. Beat the cream cheese, 1 cup sugar and vanilla with a mixer until blended. Add eggs, 1 at a time, mixing on low speed after each until blended. Pour over the crust.

3. Bake for 55 minutes at 325 degrees or until center is almost set. Loosen cake from pan; cool before removing rim. Refrigerate 4 hours before serving 16.

PUMPKIN TRIFLE

One (14-ounce) pkg. gingerbread mix (use GF) or your homemade recipe

1 (30 oz.) can pumpkin pie filling

1 (5.1 oz.) pkg. cook-and-serve vanilla pudding mix

1/2 cup brown sugar

1/3 tsp. cardamom

One 12-ounce carton Cool Whip

1/2 cup gingersnaps, optional (use GF)

1. Bake the gingerbread according to package directions; cool completely.

2. Prepare the pudding according to package directions and set aside to cool.

3. Stir in the pumpkin pie filling, sugar, and cardamom into the pudding.

4. Crumble half batch of the gingerbread in the bottom a clear trifle bowl.

5. Add 1/2 of the pudding mixture over the gingerbread. Add a layer of Cool Whip.

6. Repeat with remaining. Sprinkle top with crushed gingersnaps. Refrigerate overnight. Serves 20

PUMPKIN-SWIRL CHEESECAKE

25 ginger snap cookies; crushed (about 1-1/2 cups) (Use GF ginger snaps)

1/2 cup chopped pecans

1/4 cup butter, melted

4 pkg. (8-oz.) cream cheese, softened

1-1/3 cups sugar, divided

1 tsp. vanilla

4 eggs

1 cup canned pumpkin

1 tsp. cinnamon

1/4 tsp. nutmeg

Dash of cloves

1. Heat the oven to 325 degrees.

2. Mix crumbs, nuts, and butter; press into the bottom of a 13 x 9 pan.

3. Beat cream cheese, 1 cup sugar and vanilla until blended. Add eggs, one at a time, beating after each addition.

4. Remove 1-1/2 cups of batter and set aside. Stir remaining 1/3 cup sugar, pumpkin and spices into the remaining batter.

5. Spoon half of pumpkin batter onto crust; top with spoonfuls of the plain batter that you set aside. Repeat layers; swirl with knife.

6. Bake 45 minutes or until center is almost set. Cool completely. Refrigerate 4 hours. Serve.

LEMON CURD

2 cups sugar

1 cup fresh lemon juice (about 6 lemons)

4 large eggs

4 large yolks, beaten

1/4 cup finely grated lemon peel (about 3 lemons)

1-1/2 sticks unsalted butter, cut into pieces

1. Set a fine-mesh strainer over a medium heatproof bowl next to the stove. In a heavy saucepan, whisk together the sugar, lemon juice, eggs, yolk, and lemon peel. Add the butter and cook over medium-low heat, stirring constantly for 5 minutes.

2. Lower the heat and simmer, stirring until the mixture thickens and registers 160 degrees on an instant read thermometer, about 5 minutes.
Strain the mixture into prepared bowl; then press a sheet of plastic wrap directly onto the surface. Let cool to room temperature. Transfer to an airtight container and refrigerate for up to a month.

WAYS TO USE THE CURD
- ✓ _spread on English Muffins or toast_
- ✓ _stir into plain yogurt_
- ✓ _use as a crepe filling (crepe recipe is in the Breakfast Section)_
- ✓ _use for the stacked Lemon Crepe Cake (recipe in Cake Section)_
- ✓ _serve with pancakes and French toast_
- ✓ _fold into whipped cream_
- ✓ _make lemon chicken_
- ✓ _Enjoy!_

PRIZE CHEESE CAKE

I Love This One! It's so light, not too sweet, and fresh tasting!

12 whole graham crackers, crushed (or use GF ones)

1/2 cup melted butter

3 Tbs. powdered sugar

1 small pkg. of lemon Jello

1 cup hot water

1 can of evaporated milk, chilled overnight

1 (8 ounce) pkg. cream cheese

1 cup sugar

1 tsp. vanilla

3 Tbs. lemon juice (1 lemon)

Zest of one lemon

1. Mix 12 whole graham crackers; crushed (use GF ones), with 1/2 cup melted butter and 3 Tbs. powdered sugar. Put 2/3 of this on the bottom of a 9x13 pan. Reserve the rest for the top.

2. Mix 1 small pkg. of lemon Jello with 1 cup hot water and let cool.

3. Whip 1 can of evaporated milk that has been chilled in refrigerator overnight until thick. Set aside.

4. Cream 1-8 ounce pkg. cream cheese and then add 1 cup sugar, 1 tsp. vanilla, and 3 Tbs. lemon juice (1 lemon), and the zest, and mix. Mix in the lemon Jello mixture. Fold in the whipped canned milk.

5. Spread this on top of the crumbs and place the reserved crumbs on top.

6. Refrigerate to set for 3-4 hours. Serve. Enjoy!

BLACKBERRY-RHUBARB COBBLER

4 cups blackberries – or a combination of strawberries, raspberries and blackberries

4 cups sliced rhubarb, cut in 1-inch pieces (thaw if frozen)

2 Tbs. quick-cooking tapioca

1 Tbs. lemon juice

1 Tbs. lemon zest

1 cup sugar

1 cup old-fashioned oats (use GF)

1/4 cup flour (or gluten free flour mix)

1/2 cup brown sugar

5 Tbs. cold butter, cut into small pieces

1. Heat oven to 350 degrees. In a bowl, combine berries, rhubarb, tapioca, lemon juice and zest and sugar. Pour into a 2-quart baking dish.

2. In another bowl mix oats, flour, brown sugar and butter. Crumble in with your hands until looks like coarse crumbs. Put on the fruit.

3. Bake for 1 hour or until the topping is browned. Let stand 10 minutes before serving 8

APPLE DUMPLINGS – BEVERLY POND

A Pond Family Favorite!

Pie crust dough (or use pie sticks) for a 2 crust pie (make GF dough)

6 baking tart apples, peeled and cored

Cinnamon

1-1/2 cups water

1 cup sugar

Ice Cream, whipped cream or milk for serving

1. Make pie dough (or use pie sticks) for a 2 crust pie (make GF crust for gluten free)

2. Peel and core 6 apples

3. Roll out pie dough into a large square and cut into 6 squares (big enough to cover the apple)

4. Place an apple on each square and sprinkle the inside and outside of apple with cinnamon.

5. Lift 4 corners of dough and cover apple, Pinch dough shut.

6. Place apples into a baking dish and then sprinkle again with cinnamon.

7. To 1-1/2 cups boiling water, add 1 cup sugar and mix. Pour over the apples.

8. Bake 375 degreed for 1 hour or until tender and brown.

9. Serve with vanilla ice cream, whipped cream, or just pour a little milk or cream over it!

DESSERT DELIGHT

1 can cherry or apple pie filling

1/2 of a yellow cake mix (use a GF one)

6 Tbs. melted butter

1. Spread 1 can cherry or apple pie filling in the bottom of an 8x8-inch pan.

2. Sprinkle 1/2 of a yellow cake mix or a GF one over the top.

3. Pour on 6 Tbs. melted butter over the top.

4. Bake at 375 degrees for 40 minutes.

BLACKBERRY COBBLER

Crust:

1 cup flour (or GF mix and 1/2 tsp xanthan gum)

1/4 tsp. salt

1/3 cup shortening

3 Tbs. cold water

Filling:

3/4 cup sugar, plus additional 1 Tbs. to sprinkle on top

1/4 cup flour (or GF mix)

16 ounces frozen or 3 cups fresh blackberries

1/8 tsp. almond extract

2 Tbs. butter

1. For pastry crust: Combine 1 cup flour (or GF mix and 1/2 tsp xanthan gum), 1/4 tsp. salt, 1/3 cup shortening and beat with an electric mixer until pieces are the size of peas. Add 3 Tbs. cold water and beat until dough begins to form (15-20 seconds).

2. Form a ball and flatten. Roll into an 8-1/2 x 8-1/2-inch square and cut several slits in it.

3. In a small bowl combine the 3/4 cup sugar and 1/4 cup flour (or GF mix).

4. Place 16 ounces frozen or 3 cups fresh blackberries and 1/8 tsp. almond extract in a 2 quart square baking dish (8 x 8). Sprinkle sugar mixture over blackberries and toss to coat. Dot the 2 Tbs. butter over it.

5. Place pastry over it and sprinkle with 1 Tbs. sugar.

6. Bake for 45-50 minutes at 375 until bubbly and pastry is golden. Cool slightly. Serve warm.

LEMON SOUFFLE'

1 tsp. unsalted butter for the baking cups

5 large eggs, separated

3/4 cup sugar

1/4 cup fresh lemon juice

1 Tbs. freshly grated lemon zest

2 Tbs. powdered sugar, for dusting

Whipped cream, for garnish

1. Preheat oven to 350 degrees.

2. Butter six 2-ounce baking cups or use one 12-ounce (8x10) baking dish. Place the cups into a roasting pan. Bring a tea kettle of water to boil.

3. In a large bowl, beat the egg whites until stiff. In another bowl, beat the egg yolks until frothy and light in color, 3-4 minutes. Slowly add the sugar while still beating. Mix in lemon zest and juice.

4. Gently fold in the egg whites and pour the batter into each soufflé cup. Fill 3/4 full. Place into oven and with oven door open and carefully pour the boiling water into the roasting pan until it comes to halfway up the sides of the cups.

5. Close oven door and bake 20-25 minutes.

6. Remove pan from oven and set baking cups on wire rack to cool. Dust with powdered sugar and a dollop of whipped cream.

PUMPKIN CHEESECAKE

4 ounces gingersnap cookies, about 18 (use GF)

4 Tbs. unsalted butter

Non-stick cooking spray

4 (8 ounce) pkgs. cream cheese at room temperature

1-1/2 cups brown sugar

4 large eggs at room temperature

1/4 cup flour (use GF)

1 tsp. allspice

1 tsp. ginger

1 tsp. cinnamon, plus more

1/2 tsp. salt

1 (15 ounce) can pumpkin

3/4 cup heavy cream

1/4 cup sour cream

1 Tbs. powdered sugar

1. Heat oven to 325 degrees. In a food processor, pulse the gingersnaps until fine crumbs form (about 1 cup). Add the butter and pulse to combine.

2. Press mixture into bottom of a 9-inch springform pan (non-stick) using a straight-sided measuring cup to help press them in. Spray the sides of the pan with non-stick spray. Place on a trimmed baking sheet.

3. Using an electric mixer, beat cream cheese and brown sugar on medium until smooth, about 1 to 2 minutes. Beat in eggs, one at a time. Add in the flour, allspice, ginger, cinnamon, and salt and beat to combine.

4. Pour into prepared pan and bake until set but still slightly wobbly in the center, about 1-1/4 to 1-3/4 hours. (Tent loosely with foil on the top if top becomes too dark.)

5. Let cool completely in the pan, then refrigerate until firm, at least 2 hours. Run a knife around the edge of the cheesecake to loosen, then unmold the cheesecake.

6. Just before serving, using an electric mixer, beat the sour cream, cream, and powdered sugar until soft peaks form. Dollop this mix on the cheesecake and dust with cinnamon.

7. To Prep Ahead: The cheesecake can be baked up to 2 days in advance (do not top with the cream mixture); refrigerate, covered.

8. On Serving Day: Let sit at room temperature for 1 hour before serving. Make the sour cream mixture, dollop on the cheesecake and dust with cinnamon just before serving.

PUMPKIN-SWEET POTATO PUDDING-(CAZUELA) - SERVES 12

Yum!

1-1/2 pounds calabaza or sugar pumpkin, peeled, cut into 2-inch pieces (about 4 cups)

1-1/2 pounds boniato (sweet potatoes, or yams; peeled & cut in 2-in pieces - 4 cups)

2 Tbs. butter, divided

1 cup sugar

3/4 cup canned evaporated milk or almond milk

2 large eggs, beaten

1 cup rice flour

2 tsp. vanilla

1 tsp. cinnamon

1/2 tsp. ginger

1/2 tsp. salt

1/4 tsp. cloves

1. Bring a large pot of salted water to boil over high heat. Boil pumpkin and yams until soft, about 20-25 minutes.

2. While vegetables are cooking, grease a 9x11-inch baking dish or individual dishes with 1 Tbs. of butter.

3. Preheat oven to 350 degrees.

4. Drain the vegetables thoroughly in a colander and transfer them to a large mixing bowl. Beat them with a hand mixer until they are the consistency of lumpy mashed potatoes.

5. Beat in remaining ingredients, one by one, including the remaining tablespoon of butter.

6. Scrape batter into prepared dish and bake until a small knife inserted in the center comes out clean, about 1-1/2 hours. Cool to room temperature.

7. Invert the cazuela onto a serving dish. (The easiest way to do this is to place the plate over the cazuela and, in quick motion, flip the cazuela over.) Lift off the baking dish.

8. Serve the cazuela at room temperature, chilled or rewarmed with a dollop of cream.

THAI COCONUT STICKY RICE WITH MANGO

Rice:

2 cups glutinous rice or Thai sweet rice

2-1/2 cups water

2 Pandan leaves, fresh or frozen, optional

Coconut Topping:

1-1/2 Tbs. sugar

1 cup coconut milk

1/4 tsp. salt

Squeeze of lime

Coconut Sauce for Mixing into the Hot Rice:

3/4 cup sugar

1 15-ounce coconut milk

1-1/2 tsp. salt

Garnishes:

2 mangos; peeled, pitted, diced or sliced

2 Tbs. toasted sesame seeds

1. Combine the rice, Pandan leaves (if available) and water in a saucepan; bring to a boil, then cover and reduced heat to low. Simmer until water is absorbed, 15 to 20 minutes. Fluff with a fork and transfer to a medium bowl. The rice can also be cooked in a rice cooker until done and ready to add the coconut sauce to the hot rice.

2. Meanwhile while the rice is cooking, make the coconut topping in a saucepan. Combine the 1 cup coconut milk, 1-1/2 Tbs. sugar, and 1/4 tsp. salt. Bring to a simmer and cook over moderate heat until thickened slightly, about 10 minutes. Remove from heat and add the lime. Transfer to a small serving pitcher and let cool to room temperature.

3. Make the Coconut sauce: In a small saucepan, combine the can of coconut milk, 3/4 cup sugar, and 1-1/2 tsp. salt. Bring to a simmer.

4. Pour this hot coconut sauce over the rice in the medium bowl and fold it in gently.

5. Spoon the rice mixture into serving bowls. Top with sliced mango, toasted sesame seeds, and the coconut topping in the serving pitcher to desired consistency.

COCONUT STICKY RICE WITH MANGOS

Longer version with steamed rice

1 cup sticky rice or sweet rice found at Asian markets

1/2 cup canned full fat coconut milk, shake can to mix before opening

2 tablespoons sugar

1 teaspoon salt

1 large ripe mango, peeled, seeded and thinly sliced

Additional coconut milk, for drizzling

1/4 cup toasted coconut (optional)

Chopped peanuts for garnish

Toasted sesame seeds, (optional)

Fresh mint leaves (optional)

1. Soak rice in warm water 4 hours or overnight. Drain and rinse the rice well.

2. Pour about 1 cup of water into a saucepan, and place the rice in a steamer insert inside the saucepan. Cover tightly and steam over low to medium heat for 20-25 minutes until tender. (Add boiling water to saucepan as needed.)

3. Meanwhile, mix coconut milk, sugar and salt in small saucepan. Bring to boil on medium heat, stirring to dissolve sugar.

4. Transfer cooked sticky rice to large bowl. Gradually add coconut milk mixture, mixing well after each addition until rice is evenly coated with coconut milk.

5. Cover rice; let stand 20 to 30 minutes to allow coconut milk to be absorbed by rice.

6. To serve, arrange mango slices on 4 plates. (To cut up the mango, first cut off the bottom so it can stand upright. Slice away the skin in thin strips, until the mango is completely peeled. Cut off the flesh in slices, starting with the broad cheeks on each side, then the thinner strips that will come off either side.)

7. Spoon the 1/3 cup of coconut sticky rice onto each plate.

8. Drizzle rice with additional coconut milk. Sprinkle with toasted coconut. If desired, garnish with chopped peanuts, toasted sesame seeds and mint leaves.

ICE CREAM, ICE CREAM...

We All Scream for Ice Cream!

BEVERLY POND'S TOASTED ALMOND FUDGE ICE CREAM

This Is Our #1 Family Favorite!

4 Quart Freezer Recipe:

4 eggs

3 cups sugar

2-1/3 (1 oz.) squares melted chocolate

2 cans evaporated milk

2/3 quart cream

2/3 cup milk

1/2 tsp. salt

2 Tbs. vanilla

5-1/2 ounces almonds (raw, that have been toasted), chopped

6 Quart Freezer Recipe:

6 eggs

4-1/2 cups sugar

3 (1 oz.) squares of chocolate, 3 cans of evaporated milk

1 quart of cream

1/2 tsp. salt

3 Tbs. vanilla

8 ounces of almonds (raw, that have been toasted), chopped

1. Beat eggs until thick and _lemon_ colored. Beat in part of the sugar, then add the melted chocolate; beat. Mix in remaining sugar.

2. Add remaining ingredients except the nuts.

3. Freeze in an ice cream freezer until it just starts to freeze and you hear the change in the motor speed. Add the almonds. Finish freezing. Pack and allow it to cure for two hours.

4. _To Toast the Almonds:_ Mix almonds with just enough salad oil to coat them. Spread on a baking sheet. Bake at 400 for about 10 minutes. Watch carefully so that they do not burn. Salt

FROYO

Jessie Pond

2 cups plain Greek yogurt

1/2 cup milk

1/2 cup sugar

1 tsp. vanilla

1 Tbs. honey

1. Mix all together
2. Freeze 25 minutes in small ice cream freezer. Serves 2-3

SIX THREE'S ICE CREAM

4 Quarts:

3 cups of sugar

3 cups milk

3 cups cream

3 bananas, mashed

3 oranges, juice and zest

3 lemons, juice and zest

6 Quarts:

Use 5 cups or 5 fruits for each of the ingredients

1. Mix all together
2. Freeze in an ice cream freezer according to freezer directions.

WATERMELON ICE

1/2 cup sugar

1/4 cup watermelon or fruit gelatin powder

3/4 cup boiling water

5 cups seeded cubed watermelon

1. In a bowl, dissolve 1/2 cup sugar and 1/4 cup watermelon or fruit gelatin powder in 3/4 cup boiling water; set aside.

2. Place 5 cups seeded cubed watermelon in a blender, cover and puree. Stir in gelatin mixture. Pour into an ungreased pan. Cover and freeze overnight.

3. Remove from freezer 1 hour before serving. Spoon into paper cones or serving dishes

MOTHER'S (BERNICE GUNDRY'S) ICE CREAM SUMMER SLUSH

1/2 gallon vanilla ice cream

1/2 gallon pineapple sherbet

4 diced bananas

1 cup nuts

1-2 pkgs. of either: raspberries, blueberries, strawberries, blackberries or a mixture

1. Mix all together and freeze.

2. Take out 30 minutes to 1 hour before serving to thaw

LOW CALORIE FROZEN HOT CHOCOLATE—150 CALORIES!

1/2 cup chocolate syrup

1 cup fat-free evaporated milk

1/2 tsp. vanilla

3 cups ice cubes

1. Combine chocolate syrup, canned milk, vanilla and ice into a blender until smooth.

2. Pour into glasses and garnish with whipped topping and chocolate shavings.

✓ VARIATIONS:
✓ *Mexican Hot Chocolate: Add 1/4 tsp. cinnamon*
✓ *Peppermint Hot Chocolate: substitute 1/4 tsp. mint extract for the vanilla.*

FUDGSICLES

1 small pkg. instant chocolate pudding

1/2 cup sugar

1/2 cup heavy cream (or milk)

2 cups milk

1. Mix pudding mix with sugar milk and cream. Pour into molds and freeze.

2. Insert sticks when partially frozen.

NUTELLA CRUNCH ICE CREAM CAKE

2 cups Nutella

6 cups Rice Krispies cereal (use GF)

1 gallon vanilla ice cream

1. Place a 9 or 10 inch springform pan, as well as a very large mixing bowl in the freezer to chill.

2. In a large saucepan over low heat, combine the Nutella and Rice Krispies cereal. Mix well until the Rice Krispies are completely coated with the Nutella. Remove from heat.

3. Line a sheet pan or cookie sheet with parchment or wax paper. Pour the Nutella-Rice Krispies mixture onto the lined sheet pan and spread evenly. Then place in the freezer to chill.

4. While the coated cereal mixture is cooling, remove the ice cream from the freezer and place in the refrigerator to soften.

5. After about 30-45 minutes (you want the Nutella coated cereal to be cooled and firm but not frozen at this point) – using a fork and knife – cut the coated cereal into *bite -sized* pieces. Place back into the freezer, if necessary, until the ice cream is softened.

6. Once your ice cream is softened (it should be just softened enough to stir in the coated cereal but not so melted that it is runny), remove the Nutella-cereal pieces, the large mixing bowl and the springform pan from the freezer.

7. Reserve 2 cups of the Nutella-cereal mixture.

8. Quickly combine the ice cream and remaining coated cereal in the chilled mixing bowl, then pour the mixture into the chilled springform pan, packing it firmly so that there are no air pockets. Top the cake with the reserved Nutella-cereal mixture.

9. Cover with plastic wrap and place the springform pan back into the freezer for at least 4-6 hours, or until firm.

10. 1Remove the cake from the freezer about 30-45 minutes before serving and place in the refrigerator to soften a bit.

11. 1When ready to serve, place the cake on a platter or cake stand and remove the sides of the springform pan. Cut and serve immediately.

MINT OREO ICE CREAM PIE/CAKE

1/2 gallon of mint chocolate ice cream, softened

1 pkg. of Oreo cookies, crushed (use GF)

1. Layer 2/3 of the crushed Oreos in the bottom of a pie pan or baking dish.

2. Top with ice cream and the rest of the Oreos. Freeze until firm.

3. Serve with Hot Fudge sauce, if desired.

CHOCOLATE CHIP ICE CREAM PIE

1/2 cup chocolate syrup

1/3 cup semisweet chocolate chips

2 cups crisp rice cereal (GF)

1/4 cup sour cream

1 quart chocolate chip or mint chip ice cream, softened

1. Coat bottom and sides of 8-inch pie plate with butter.

2. Combine chocolate syrup and chips in small glass bowl. Microwave on High until hot, about 45 seconds. Stir until smooth. Reserve 1/4 cup of mixture.

3. Combine remaining chocolate in a medium bowl with the rice cereal and mix to coat. Press into pie plate on bottom and up the sides. Freeze until firm, about 15 minutes.

4. Combine reserved 1/4 cup chocolate mixture and sour cream in a small bowl and mix well. Spread half of ice cream in pie plate. Drizzle with half of sour cream mixture. Top with remaining ice cream and drizzle with remaining sour cream mixture.

5. Freeze pie, covered, until firm, about 1 hour.

DESSERT SAUCES

HOT FUDGE SAUCE

1 cup heavy cream

2 Tbs. light corn syrup

12-ounces semisweet chocolate

2 tsp. vanilla

1. In a medium saucepan, combine the cream and corn syrup. Bring to boil over medium heat.

2. Remove from the heat, add the chocolate and whisk until melted; stir in vanilla.

3. Serve or pour into a jar and let cool completely before refrigerating for up to 2 weeks.

4. Warm in the microwave or in a small pan before serving.

FUDGE SAUCE

3 ounces semisweet or dark chocolate chips (1/2 cup)

1 can sweetened condensed milk

1/4 cup butter

1. In a saucepan, heat butter and condensed milk over medium-low heat until butter is melted. Add the chips and stir until chocolate is melted.

2. Remove from heat. This can store for 2 weeks in refrigerator.

HOT FUDGE SAUCE

Marie Hofmann

1 cup semi-sweet chocolate chips

1/3 cup butter or margarine

1 oz. (1 square) baking chocolate, broken up

1-1/4 cups evaporated milk (10 oz.)

2 cups powdered sugar

1 tsp. vanilla

1. In an 8 cup glass measuring cup or bowl (use this size or it will boil over), microwave all chocolate and butter for 1-1/2 minutes on Power 8 (medium high).

2. Stir until all is melted and smooth. Whisk in evaporated milk, powdered sugar, and vanilla. Microwave mixture on Power 8 again for 10 minutes until thickened. Stir.

3. If not thickened, microwave for a couple more minutes. All microwaves are different and you may need to experiment on just how long to microwave.

4. Serve hot over ice cream. Refrigerate and reheat as needed.

FRESH RASPBERRY SAUCE FOR ICE CREAM, CHEESECAKES, ETC.

1/2 pint of fresh raspberries, washed

1/2 cup sugar

1/4 cup water

1/2 cup raspberry jam

1. Combine the above and cook for a few minutes and then add 1/2 cup raspberry jam.

2. Blend in a food processor. Serve over ice cream, cheesecake, etc.

CARAMEL SAUCE

1 cup brown sugar, firmly packed

1/2 cup light corn syrup

1/2 cup butter

1/2 cup milk or cream

1/2 tsp. vanilla

1. In a saucepan mix all ingredients together and cook slowly, stirring constantly.

2. Bring to a boil and cook for 5 minutes. Cool. Serve over ice cream or cake.

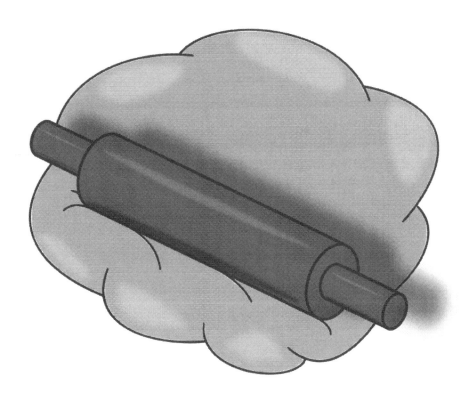

PIES, CRUSTS, AND MORE PIES

LIBBY'S FAMOUS PUMPKIN PIE RECIPE

(For 2 (9-inch) pies, double this recipe, pour into 2 pastry shells and bake as directed.)

2 eggs

1/2 cup Libby's pumpkin

3/4 cup sugar

2 tsp. salt

1 tsp. cinnamon

1/2 tsp. ginger

1/4 tsp. cloves

1-2/3 cups evaporated milk, large can

1 9-inch unbaked pie shell

1. Mix filling in the order given. Pour into pie shell.

2. Bake in a preheated hot oven (425) for 15 minutes. Reduce temperature to moderate (350) and continue baking for 45 minutes or until knife inserted into center of pie filling come out clean. Cool.

3. Garnish with whipped cream.

MARY GUNDRY'S CUSTARD OR PIE

No Crust Needed!

4 eggs

1/3 to 1/2 cup sugar, or more to taste

2-1/2 cups milk

1/4 tsp. salt

1/4 to 1/2 tsp. nutmeg, to taste

1 tsp. vanilla

1. Beat 4 eggs; add 1/3 cup sugar, 2-1/2 cups milk, 1/4 tsp. salt, 1/2 tsp. nutmeg, 1 tsp. vanilla

2. Stir and pour into square glass baking pan. Sprinkle with nutmeg. Place baking dish in a larger pan of cold water to a depth of 1/4" in oven.

3. Bake at 350 for about 30-40 minutes or until set when knife is inserted. Cool.

Option: This can be prepared and cooked in an un-baked pastry shell on the oven rack at 350 degrees for 35 to 40 minutes. Bake leftover custard in custard cups.

MOTHER'S (BERNICE GUNDRY'S) PECAN PIE

3/4 cup light corn syrup

3 eggs

2/3 cup sugar

1 tsp. white vinegar

2 Tbs. butter, melted

1 tsp. vanilla

1/8 tsp. salt

1 cup pecans, halved or chopped

1 prepared pie crust shell

1. Beat eggs and then add sugar and mix until dissolved into eggs.

2. Add the rest of ingredients except pecans. Mix well. Stir in the pecans.

3. Tip: Add 1 Tbs. of flour to the filling mix if using a store bought crust.

4. Pour into pastry shell. Bake at 400 degrees for 5 minutes. Reduce heat to 350 and bake 30-35 minutes longer (or cook 350 for 45 min.)

5. Outer edge of pie should be set and center slightly soft. Serves 8-10

GLAZED FRESH STRAWBERRY PIE

1 baked 9-inch pastry shell

3 pints strawberries, washed and hulled

1 cup sugar

3-1/2 Tbs. corn starch

1/2 cup water

A few drops of red food coloring

Whipped cream

1. Mash 1 pint strawberries. Mix sugar and corn starch in a 3-quart saucepan.

2. Stir in water and mashed berries. Cook over medium heat, stirring constantly, until mixture comes to a boil and boils 2 minutes. Remove from heat. Stir in food coloring. Cool.

3. Fold remaining 2 pints of berries into cooked mixture. Pile into pastry shell. Chill.

4. Serve with shipped cream.

JANEEN'S AND NICHOLEEN'S APPLE CRISP

1-2 quarts canned apple pie filling (recipe below) or 2 - 3 cans from store

1 cup sugar

2 cups flour (or GF mix & 1 tsp. xanthan gum)

1/2 tsp. cinnamon

1/2 tsp. nutmeg

1 cup butter

Ice cream or whipped cream to serve with, optional

1. Mix the flour, sugar, cinnamon, and nutmeg above and cut in the butter until crumbly either with pastry blender or hand mixer. Sprinkle 1/3 of mixture in the bottom of a 9x13 pan.

2. Pour over the apple filling and then sprinkle with remainder of topping.

3. Bake at 375 degrees until golden brown – about 45 minutes.

4. Great served with ice cream or whipped cream.

JANEEN'S APPLE PIE FILLING

4-1/2 cups sugar

1 cup cornstarch

2 tsp. cinnamon

1/4 tsp. cloves

1/4 tsp. nutmeg

1 tsp. salt

10 cups water

3 tsp. lemon juice

Apples; peeled, cored, and sliced

1. Use an apple-peeler-corer to prepare apples. Fill 7 quart jars with sliced apples.

2. Cook the above ingredients except the apples until thick. Pour over the sliced apples in the jars.

3. Seal and process 20 minutes in water bath canner. Makes 7 quarts

APPLE PIE

6 to 8 tart apples, pared, cored, and thinly sliced (6 cups)--if apples are not tart, sprinkle on 1 Tbs. lemon juice

3/4 to 1 cup sugar

2 Tbs. flour (GF)

1/2 to 1 tsp. cinnamon

Dash of nutmeg

2 Tbs. butter

Pastry for double-crust pie (use GF) or 1 crust and Crumb topping, below

1. Combine sugar, flour, spices, and a dash of salt; mix in the apples. Line a 9-inch pie plate with pastry.

2. Fill in with apple mixture; dot with butter. Adjust top crust and make slits to let steam escape. Seal the crust.

3. Sprinkle with sugar and bake at 400 degrees for 50 minutes or until done.

CRUMB TOPPING FOR APPLE PIE

1/2 cup flour (use GF mix)

1/4 cup sugar

1/4 cup butter

1. Combine flour and sugar; cut in the butter until crumbly.

2. Top the apples in the pie crust and bake at 400 degree for 40-50 minutes

EASY CUSTARD PIE

3/4 cup sugar

1/2 tsp. salt

1/2 cup Bisquick or GF Bisquick mix

1/4 cup butter

4 eggs

2 cups milk

1-1/2 tsp. vanilla

Nutmeg, optional

1/2 cup coconut, optional

1. Measure directly into a blender: 3/4 cup sugar, 1/2 tsp. salt, 1/2 cup Bisquick or GF Bisquick mix, 1/4 cup butter, 4 eggs, 2 cups milk, and 1-1/2 tsp. vanilla

2. Blend for a full 3 minutes. Don't cheat on this or it won't work. Pour into a 9-inch pie pan. You may sprinkle with nutmeg to taste and 1/2 cup coconut before baking, if desired.

3. Bake at 350 degrees for 40 minutes or until golden brown. Be careful to not over bake or the custard will be too sturdy.

BANANA CREAM PIE OR COCONUT CREAM PIE

Your favorite baked and cooled 9-inch pie crust

3 bananas, sliced

Vanilla cream pie filling (recipe below) or 1 pkg. banana cream instant or cooked pudding made to pie directions

Whipped cream for garnish

1. Slice the bananas into the baked pie crust. Top with the Vanilla Cream Pie Filling.

2. Chill until serving time. Serve with dollops of whipped cream on top.

3. *Option:* For Coconut Cream Pie, add 1 cup of flaked coconut to the Vanilla Cream Pie Filling and garnish with whipped cream and 3 Tbs. more coconut.

VANILLA CREAM PIE FILLING

3/4 cup sugar

1/3 cup flour or 3 Tbs. cornstarch (I use cornstarch for GF or non-GF)

1/4 tsp. salt

2 cups milk

3 slightly beaten egg yolks

2 Tbs. butter

1 tsp. vanilla

1. In a saucepan, combine the sugar, cornstarch or flour and salt. Gradually add in the milk.

2. Cook and stir over medium heat until bubbly. Cook and stir for 2 minutes.

3. Remove from heat and stir a small amount of the hot mixture in the beaten egg yolks; immediately return yolks to the hot mixture; cook 2 minutes, stirring constantly.

4. Remove from heat and add the butter and vanilla.

5. Pour into the cooled pie shell. Place a piece of waxed paper on the top of hot pie filling to prevent a skin from forming. Refrigerate until serving.

CHERRY CHEESE CAKE PIE

1 crumb crust (GF)

1 pkg. 8-ounce cream cheese, room temperature

1 can of Eagle Brand Condensed Milk

1/3 cup lemon juice

1 tsp. vanilla

1 can prepared cherry or other flavor of your choice pie filling

1. Soften cream cheese and whip until fluffy. Add milk gradually and beat until well blended.

2. Add lemon juice and vanilla and blend. Pour into crust.

3. Chill 2-3 hours before topping with pie filling of your choice and serving.

LEMON MERINGUE PIE

1 baked 9-inch pie crust (GF)

1/2 cup sugar

1/4 cup corn starch

1/4 tsp. salt

1-1/2 cups water

3 egg yolks

1/2 cup sugar

2 Tbs. butter

1/3 cup lemon juice

1-1/2 tsp. grated lemon rind/zest

3 egg whites

6 Tbs. sugar

1. Combine 1/2 cup sugar, corn starch, and salt in double boiler top. Gradually blend in water. Cook over boiling water stirring constantly, until thickened. Cover and cook an additional 10 minutes, stirring occasionally.

2. Meanwhile, beat together egg yolks and 1/2 cup sugar. Blend in a little of the hot mixture in double boiler top. Cook over boiling water 2 minutes, stirring constantly, and adding the egg yolk mix. Remove from boiling water. Add butter, lemon juice, lemon rind. Cool. Pour into baked shell.

3. Beat egg whites until foamy. Add sugar 1 Tbs. at a time beating well after each addition. Continue beating until stiff peaks form when beaters are raised. Spread meringue around edge to touch all edges and then fill in the center.

4. Bake until meringue is lightly browned, 15-20 minutes at 350 or for 5 minutes at 42Cool and room temperature and keep away from drafts.

FROZEN PEACH PIES

Makes 4 (9-Inch Pies)

4 quarts peeled and sliced peaches

3-1/2 cups sugar

2 tsp. fruit fresh

1/2 cup plus 2 Tbs. Minute Tapioca

1/4 to 1/3 c. lemon juice

1 tsp. salt

1. Line 4 pie tins with foil and parchment paper.

2. Pour in filling, freeze----after frozen, remove tins, and place in freezer zip-lock bags.

TO PREPARE
- ✓ *Remove filling from the freezer, remove foil, place filling in pie crust, top with another crust or crumb crust. Bake at 400 degrees until bubbly (frozen will take longer)…..no need to thaw.*
- ✓ *These can also be used for peach cobbler – use two peach fillings in a 9 x 13 pan. Top with a crumb crust mix and bake at 400 degrees until bubbly.*

RHUBARB PIE

4 cups rhubarb; cut in 1-inch slices

1-2/3 cups sugar

1/3 cup flour (or use 3 Tbs. quick-cooking Tapioca for GF)

Dash of salt

Crust for a 2-crust pie - your favorite recipe

2 Tbs. butter

1. Mix rhubarb, sugar, flour, and salt. Place the rhubarb mixture into the prepared pie crust.

2. Dot with 2 Tbs. butter

3. Top with other crust, cut in some slits, seal, and flute.

4. Bake at 400 degrees for 50 minutes

STRAWBERRY-RHUBARB PIE

3 cups (1 pound) rhubarb; cut into 1/2-inch pieces

1 cup sliced strawberries

1-1/2 cups sugar

3 Tbs. quick-cooking Tapioca

1/4 tsp. salt

1/4 tsp. nutmeg

1 2-crust pastry shell

1 Tbs. butter

1. Mix all together except the pastry shell and butter and let stand 20 minutes

2. Meanwhile, prepare a 2-crust pastry shell or lattice top pie 9-inch crust

3. Pour fruit mixture into the prepared pastry and dot with 1 Tbs. butter

4. Adjust top crust. Bake at 400 degrees for 35 to 40 minutes.

RHUBARB CUSTARD PIE

Goodness in Rich, Creamy Custard!

1 unbaked 9-inch pie shell (GF)

Filling:

1-1/2 pounds rhubarb (4 cups cut in slices)

1 Tbs. lemon juice

3/4 cup sugar

1/8 tsp. salt

2 Tbs. flour (GF mix)

Topping:

3 eggs

1/4 tsp. nutmeg

1 cup heavy cream

2 Tbs. sugar

2 Tbs. butter, melted

1. *Filling:* In a bowl, combine rhubarb, cut in 1/4-inch slices, sugar, flour, lemon juice and salt. Toss to mix and turn into pie shell. Bake 20 minutes at 400 degrees.

2. *Topping:* Beat eggs slightly in a bowl; stir in cream, butter and nutmeg and blend. Pour over hot rhubarb in pie shell. Bake 10 minutes; sprinkle with the sugar and then bake 10 minutes more until top is browned. Cool on rack before serving.

FAVORITE FRUIT CRUNCH

5 cups fresh peaches, apples, rhubarb, etc.

1/2 cup sugar

1 tsp. cinnamon

1/2 tsp. nutmeg

Crumb Topping:

1 cup flour (GF mix or 2/3 cup rice flour, 1/4 cup potato starch, 2 Tbs. tapioca starch and 1/2 tsp. Xanthan)

1-1/2 tsp. baking powder

1/8 tsp. salt

1/2 cup brown sugar or white

1 egg, beaten

1/2 cup butter

1/2 cup nuts, chopped, if desired

To serve:

Ice cream or whipped topping to serve with, optional

1. Slice peaches or fruit of choice and place in bottom of a 2 quart baking dish (9 x 9). Mix 1/2 cup sugar, cinnamon, and nutmeg; sprinkle over the fruit.

2. *Make Crumb Topping*: In a medium bowl, combine flour, baking powder, salt, and sugar. Add egg and beat with hand mixer until crumbly. Sprinkle over the fruit.

3. Melt butter and drizzle over top of crumb mixture. Sprinkle with 1/2 cup chopped nuts, if desired.

4. Bake at 350 degrees for 40 to 45 minutes or until lightly browned and fruit tests done.

5. Serve with ice cream or whipped topping.

ALMOND BERRY TART

Crust:

1⁄2 cup ground, unblanched almonds

1-1⁄2 cups flour (use GF mix with 1 tsp xanthan gum)

1⁄2 tsp. salt

1 tsp. sugar

1-1⁄2 sticks cold butter

1⁄4 cup ice water

Filling:

2 cups blueberries

1 cup raspberries

1 cup blackberries

Zest of 1 lemon

1⁄2 cup sugar

2 Tbs. flour (GF)

Sliced almonds and granulated sugar for garnish

1. To make the crust, combine the ground almonds, flour, salt and sugar by pulsing in a food processor. Add butter, and pulse until the size of peas. With machine running, quickly add water; stop the machine when the dough begins to come together.

2. Remove the dough, and knead once or twice to make sure it is well mixed. Wrap in plastic and refrigerate until firm, at least 1 hour.

3. Preheat oven to 375 degrees. In a medium bowl, combine the filling ingredients and mix well.

4. On a well-floured (GF) surface, roll the dough into a rough circle about 1⁄8" to 1⁄4" thick and 14 inch diameter. Transfer to parchment lined baking sheet; if dough has softened too much to handle then chill again.

5. Place berry mixture in an even layer, leaving a 2 to 3-inch border. Fold the border 2 to 3-inches of dough over the berries. Gently brush exposed dough with water and sprinkle with sliced almonds and sugar.

6. Bake in center of oven until golden brown and berries are bubbling, about 45 minutes. Remove and let cool 1 hour before serving. Serve with a dollop of ice cream! Serves 6-8

PIE CRUSTS...

OIL PIE CRUST

2 cups flour (GF mix)

1-1/2 tsp. salt

1/2 cup oil

5 Tbs. cold water or milk

1. Mix with a fork until blended.

2. Divide dough into 2 pieces and roll between sheets of waxed paper. Transfer to pans.

3. Makes 2 single pie crusts or 1 double.

4. To bake a single crust, bake at 400 degrees for 10-15 minutes. Prick with a fork before baking a single crust.

CREAM CHEESE PASTRY DOUGH

8 Tbs. unsalted butter, room temperature

4 ounces cream cheese, room temperature

1/4 cup heavy cream

1-1/2 cups flour plus 2 Tbs. for rolling out dough (use GF)

1/2 tsp. salt

1. Mix butter, cream cheese and cream in food processor, mixer or by hand.

2. Add flour and salt. Process until dough holds together in a ball. Turn dough out onto a well-floured surface. Divide dough in 2 pieces and wrap in plastic wrap for at least 30 minutes before rolling out. If dough has been chilled overnight, take out 15 minutes before rolling.

3. Roll out dough and form a 12-inch circle. Place in pie pan.

4. Makes 2 crusts or 1 double-crust pie.

CRUMB PIE CRUST

Gluten Free

> **1/3 cup butter**
>
> **3/4 cup brown or white rice flour (or use regular flour for non-GF)**
>
> **1/4 cup brown sugar**
>
> **1/2 tsp. vanilla**
>
> **1/4 tsp. xanthan gum**
>
> **1/3 cup chopped pecans or walnuts**

1. Combine all ingredients but the butter. Cut in the butter with a pastry cutter.

2. Spread crumbs in one 9-inch pie pan and shape with a spoon to cover sides and bottom.

3. Bake in 350 oven for 15 minutes.

4. Let cool and then pour in the filling. Great to use instead of graham cracker crusts!

QUICK N' EASY PIE CRUST

Gluten Free

> **1/2 cup shortening**
>
> **1/8 tsp. salt**
>
> **1-1/4 cups rice flour - or use regular flour**
>
> **3 Tbs. cold water**

1. In a medium bowl, cut in shortening into rice flour and salt until crumbly.

2. Add water and work into a soft ball. Place dough in pie pan and press to the shape of the pan. Prick with fork 5 times on bottom to prevent buckling.

3. Bake in 400 oven for 12-15 minutes.

INGREDIENT GLUTEN-FREE PIE CRUST

Fill with your favorite gluten-free pie, tart, fruit, or cheesecake!

1-1/4 cup almond meal (or finely ground almonds, unblanched)

1/3 cup butter

3 Tbs. sugar

1. Preheat oven to 350 F. Melt butter and combine with almond meal and sugar.

2. Mix well until butter is absorbed. Spread into 8" pie pan, pushing into corners and on edges. Bake for 10 minutes; until it is slightly browned. Cool.

CRUMB TOPPING FOR APPLE PIES OR COBBLERS

For a 9 x 13 baking dish:

2 cups flour (GF)

1 cup sugar

1 cup butter

For a pie:

1/2 cup flour (GF)

1/4 cup sugar

1/4 cup butter

1. Mix the 3 ingredients until crumbly

2. Then put on top of pie or cobbler.

GINGERSNAP COOKIE PIE CRUST

1-1/2 cups fine gingersnap cookie crumbs (use GF)

1/4 cup softened butter

1. Mix the above and press firmly into a buttered 9-inch pie plate.

2. Bake at 375 degrees for about 9 minutes. Cool

GRAHAM-CRACKER PIE CRUST

1-1/2 cups fine graham-cracker crumbs (use GF)

1/4 cup sugar

6 Tbs. butter, melted

1. Combine the above and press into a 9-inch pie plate.

2. Bake at 375 degrees for 6 to 9 minutes or until the edges are browned.

CHOCOLATE-WAFER OR VANILLA-WAFER PIE CRUST

1-1/2 cups fine vanilla-wafer or chocolate-wafer crumbs (use GF wafers)

6 Tbs. butter, melted

1. Combine the above and press into a 9-inch pie plate.

2. Chill until set.

GLUTEN FREE: SUBSTITUTIONS, FLOURS, MIXES, ETC.

Reminder: Always make sure your work surfaces, utensils, pans and tools are free of gluten. Always read product labels. Manufacturers can change product formulations without notice. When in doubt, do not buy or use a product before contacting the manufacturer for verification that the product is free of gluten.

CONVERSION CHART: WHEAT TO GLUTEN FREE

WHEAT FLOUR	RICE FLOUR	POTATO STARCH	TAPIOCA STARCH	XANTHAN GUM
3-1/2 cups	= 2-1/2 cups	2/3 cup	1/3 cup	1-3/4 tsp.
3 cup	= 2 cups	2/3 cup	1/3 cup	1-1/2 tsp.
2-1/2 cups	= 1-3/4 cups	1/2 cup	1/4 cup	1-1/4 tsp.
2 cup	= 1-1/2 cups	1/3 cup	1/4 cup	1 tsp.
1-1/2 cups	= 1 cup	1/3 cup	1/4 cup	3/4 tsp.
1 cup	= 2/3 cup	1/4 cup	2 Tbs.	1/2 tsp.
3/4 cup	= 1/2 cup	3 Tbs.	1 Tbs.	1/3 tsp.
1/2 cup	= 1/3 cup	3 Tbs.	1 Tbs.	1/4 tsp.
1/3 cup	= 1/4 cup	1 Tbs.	1 Tbs.	1/8 tsp.

OPTIONAL OTHER WAYS TO CONVERT RECIPES:

Increase Baking Powder and Soda:

- If a recipe calls for 1 tsp. baking powder: Use 1-1/2 tsp. Baking Powder

- If a recipe calls for 1 tsp. Soda: Use 1 tsp. Soda and 1/2 tsp. Baking Powder

Add or increase eggs in cakes, cookies, muffins, and breads:

- If a recipe calls for 1 egg, increase to 2 eggs and decrease liquid by 2 Tbs.

- If a recipe calls for 2 eggs, increase to 3 eggs and decrease liquid by 2 Tbs.

Baking Booster: Use Baking Booster in place of Xanthan gum, if desired.

Brown Rice Flour: Brown rice flour is less grainy in recipes white rice flour

<u>A Rule Of Thumb To Use When Baking GF Desserts, Cookies, Etc.:</u> Use 1/2 Featherlight Mix And 1/2 Of Another GF Mix And 1 Tsp. Xanthan Gum For Every 2 Cups Of GF Flours.

THE GLUTEN FREE FLOUR MIXES

These mixes are great to keep in the pantry for use.

BETTE HAGMAN'S FEATHERLIGHT MIX

My Favorite!

1 cup rice flour

1 cup cornstarch

1 cup tapioca starch

1 Tbs. potato flour (*not* potato starch flour)

1. Combine and mix well.

2. Store this in an air-tight container on your pantry shelf.

BETTE HAGMAN'S GF MIX

6 cup rice flour

2 cups potato starch flour (*not* potato flour)

1 cup tapioca starch

1. Combine and mix well.

2. Store this in an air-tight container on your pantry shelf.

BETTE HAGMAN'S FRENCH BREAD MIX

3-1/2 cup white rice flour

2-1/2 cup tapioca flour

2 Tbs. xanthan gum

2 (7 gram) packets unflavored gelatin

2 Tbs. egg replacer

1/4 cup sugar

1. Combine and mix well.

2. Store this in an air-tight container on your pantry shelf.

ALL PURPOSE GLUTEN FREE FLOUR MIX

4 cups tapioca flour or starch

2 cups potato starch

1 cup white rice flour

1 cup corn flour

1/2 cup millet flour

1. Combine all and mix very well.

2. This mix stores for up to 6 weeks in an air-tight container on the pantry shelf.

SUBSTITUTION SOLUTIONS FOR GF & DAIRY-FREE

MILK

Replace 1 cup cow's milk with one of the following:

- 1 cup soy milk (plain)
- 1 cup rice milk
- 1 cup fruit juice
- 1 cup water
- 1 cup coconut milk
- 1 cup goat's milk, if tolerated
- 1 cup hemp milk

BUTTERMILK

Replace 1 cup buttermilk with one of the following:

- 1 cup soy milk + 1 tablespoon lemon juice or 1 tablespoon white vinegar (Let stand until slightly thickened.)
- 1 cup coconut milk
- 7/8 cup rice milk
- 7/8 cup fruit juice
- 7/8 cup water

YOGURT

Replace 1 cup yogurt with one of the following:

- 1 cup soy yogurt or coconut yogurt
- 1 cup soy sour cream
- 1 cup unsweetened applesauce
- 1 cup fruit puree

BUTTER

Replace 8 tablespoons (1 stick) butter with one of the following:

- 8 tablespoons (1 stick) Fleischmann's unsalted margarine
- 8 tablespoons Earth Balance (Non-Dairy) Buttery Spread
- 8 tablespoons Spectrum Organic Shortening
- 8 tablespoons vegetable or olive oil

For reduced fat:

- 6 tablespoons unsweetened applesauce + 2 tablespoons fat of choice

EGGS

Replace 1 large egg with one of the following:

- 3 tablespoons unsweetened applesauce (or other fruit puree) + 1 teaspoon baking powder
- 1 tablespoon flax meal or chia seed plus 3 tablespoons hot water. (Let stand, stirring occasionally, about 10 minutes or until thick. Use without straining.)
- Egg Replacer, according to package directions
- 4 tablespoons pureed silken tofu + 1 teaspoon baking powder
- Replacing more than two eggs will change the integrity of a recipe. For recipes that call for a lot of eggs, like a quiche, use pureed silken tofu.
- Because egg substitutions add moisture, you may have to increase baking times slightly.

NOTE:
✓ *To replace one egg white, dissolve 1 tablespoon plain agar powder into 1 tablespoon water. Beat, chill for 15 minutes and beat again.*

NUTS

Replace tree nuts or peanuts with an equal amount of the following:

- Toasted coconut
- Sunflower seeds
- Toasted sesame seeds (use only 2 to 3 tablespoons)
- Crushed cornflakes
- Crushed crispy rice cereal
- Crushed potato chips
- Pumpkin seeds

GLUTEN-FREE FLOUR SUBSTITUTIONS

To make a flour blend, thoroughly combine all ingredients. Store this in a covered container in the refrigerator until used. This can also be stored on the pantry shelf for shortened periods of time. You can double or triple these recipes to make as much flour mix as you need.

NOTE:
- ✓ *If you purchase a commercial flour blend, read the ingredient list carefully. Some blends contain salt and xanthan or guar gum. If so, there is no need to add more.*

ALL-PURPOSE FLOUR BLEND

Use this blend for all your gluten-free baking.

- 1/2 cup rice flour
- 1/4 cup tapioca starch/flour
- 1/4 cup cornstarch or potato starch

Each cup contains 436 calories, 1g total fat,

0g saturated fat, 0g trans-fat, 0mg cholesterol, 99g carbohydrate, 3mg sodium, 2g fiber, 5g protein

276

HIGH-FIBER FLOUR BLEND

This high-fiber blend works for breads, pancakes, snack bars and cookies that contain chocolate, warm spices, raisins or other fruits. It is not suited to delicately flavored recipes, such as sugar cookies, crepes, cream puffs, birthday cakes or cupcakes.

1 cup brown rice flour or sorghum Flour

1/2 cup Teff flour (preferably light)

1/2 cup millet flour or Montina® flour

2/3 cup tapioca starch/flour

1/3 cup cornstarch or potato starch

Each cup contains 428 calories; 2g total fat, 0g saturated fat, 0g trans-fat, 0mg cholesterol, 92g carbohydrate, 19mg sodium, 5g fiber, 8g protein.

HIGH-PROTEIN FLOUR BLEND

This nutritious blend works best in baked goods that require elasticity, such as wraps and pie crusts.

1-1/4 cups bean flour (your choice), chickpea flour or soy flour

1 cup arrowroot starch, cornstarch or potato starch

1 cup tapioca starch/flour

1 cup white or brown rice flour

Each cup contains 588 calories; 3g total fat, 0g saturated fat, 0g trans-fat, 0mg cholesterol, 128g carbohydrate, 24mg sodium, 6g fiber, 11g protein.

SELF-RISING FLOUR BLEND

Use this blend for muffins, scones, cakes, cupcakes or any recipe that uses baking powder for leavening.

1-1/4 cups white sorghum flour

1-1/4 cups white rice flour

1/2 cup tapioca starch/flour

2 teaspoons xanthan or guar gum

4 teaspoons baking powder

1/2 teaspoon salt

*Each cup contains 514 calories; 3g total fat, 0g
saturated fat, 0g trans-fat, 0mg cholesterol, 113g carbohydrate, 1163mg sodium, 8g fiber, 10g protein.*

Nutritional analyses of recipes are based on data supplied by the U.S. Department of Agriculture and certain food companies. Nutrient amounts are approximate due to variances in product brands, manufacturing and actual preparation

GENERAL GUIDELINES FOR USING XANTHAN OR GUAR GUM

Gum (xanthan or guar) is the key to successful gluten-free baking. It provides the binding needed to give the baked product proper elasticity, keeping it from crumbling.

- Add 1/2 teaspoon xanthan or guar gum per cup of flour blend to make cakes, cookies, bars, muffins and other quick breads.

- Add 1 teaspoon per cup of flour blend to make yeast bread, pizza dough or other baked items that call for yeast.

<u>NOTE:</u>

✓ *If you purchase a commercial flour blend, read the ingredient list carefully. Some blends contain salt and xanthan or guar gum. If so, there is no need to add more.*

TO MAKE ALMOND OR OAT FLOUR

1 cup whole, unblanched almonds or 1 cup quick oats

1. Measure 1 cup whole, un-blanched almonds or 1 cup whole or quick oats and place them into a clean blender, food processor or coffee grinder and pulse until fine.

2. Don't over-blend or you could end up with almond butter!

3. Sift the meal to separate fine and coarse pieces. Process this until fine.

4. Use what is needed and refrigerate the rest and use within a month or freeze for longer storage.

GLUTEN FREE FLOUR SUBSTITUTIONS

This chart will help you know what flours are interchangeable if you run out of one as you are cooking. While they are not identical, they have comparable baking characteristics and a similar way they build the structure in a recipe. Items might taste a little different though.

- Neutral (Light) Flours - Brown rice flour, white rice flour, sorghum flour, sweet rice flour, and corn flour can be interchanged.

- High-Protein Flours - Amaranth flour, buckwheat flour, chickpea flour, millet flour, oat flour, quinoa flour, sorghum flour, and Teff flour can be interchanged.

- High-Fiber Flours - Amaranth flour, buckwheat flour, chickpea flour, corn flour, mesquite flour, oat flour, quinoa flour and Teff flour can be interchanged.

- Stabilizers (add texture and moisture) - Almond flour, coconut flour, flax seed meal, ground chia seed, oat bran, and potato flour can be interchanged.

- Starches - Arrowroot powder, cornstarch, Kudzu root starch or Kuzu, potato starch, sweet potato flour, and tapioca starch or flour can be interchanged.

- Gums - Agar powder, carrageenan, gelatin powder, guar gum, locust bean gum, psyllium husk, and xanthan gum can be interchanged.

GLUTEN-FREE CREAM OF MUSHROOM SOUP AND MASTER MIX

Homemade gluten-free cream soups aren't hard to make and gluten-free sweet rice flour is an excellent thickener! Gluten-free cream of mushroom soup takes less than 20 minutes to make and the creamy fresh flavor is so worth it!

8 ounces fresh sliced mushrooms

1/4 cup finely diced sweet onions

2 minced garlic cloves

3 tablespoons butter

4 tablespoons gluten-free sweet rice flour

1 cup low sodium gluten-free chicken broth

1 cup light cream or whole milk

1/2 teaspoon salt or to taste

1/4 teaspoon pepper or to taste

Garnish with fresh sliced basil (optional)

1. Saute mushrooms, onions and garlic with butter in a 3 quart saucepan over medium heat for about 3 minutes. Sprinkle gluten-free sweet rice flour over vegetables and stir to blend the rice flour into the mixture. Continue to cook vegetables with sweet rice flour while stirring for 2 minutes.

2. Gradually stir in gluten-free chicken broth and stir to blend. Add cream or milk and continue to cook over medium heat until soup thickens. Season this with salt and pepper, to taste.

REMINDER:
- ✓ *Always make sure your work surfaces, utensils, pans and tools are free of gluten.*
- ✓ *Always read product labels. Manufacturers can change product formulations without notice.*
- ✓ *When in doubt, do not buy or use a product before contacting the manufacturer for verification that the product is free of gluten.*

GLUTEN FREE CREAM SOUP MASTER-MIX

This is a low-fat, low cost gluten free master-mix recipe for creamed condensed soup. Great to keep on hand in your pantry!

2 cups instant dry milk or Dairy Free Instant Powder

1 cup cornstarch

3 Tbs. chicken bouillon granules

2 Tbs. instant minced onion

1/2 tsp. thyme leaves, crushed

1/4 tsp. pepper

1. Mix together and store in an airtight container.

2. Yield: 3-1/2 cups

CREAM SOUP USING THE MASTER MIX

One recipe is equal to one can (10 ¾-ounce) condensed soup:

1/3 cup Cream Soup Mix (see above)

1-1/4 cup water or milk

2 Tbs. mayonnaise or butter blended in (optional)

1. Combine soup mix and water or milk in a small saucepan.

2. Bring to boil and stir until thick.

HOW TO USE THIS MASTER-MIX SOUP RECIPE IN COOKING:

For a Casserole:

Combine soup mix and water/milk and add to casserole. It will thicken as it cooks and cools after.

VARIATIONS:
- ✓ *Cream of Mushroom--add 1 (4-ounce can) drained mushrooms (could use some of liquid for flavor)*
- ✓ *Cream of Chicken—add 1/2 cup cooked and diced chicken*
- ✓ *Cream of Celery—Saute 1/3 cup chopped celery in butter until tender and add to mix..*
- ✓ *Cheese Soup Condensed—Stir in 1/2 to 2/3 cup grated cheddar cheese after mayonnaise is blended in.*

GLUTEN FREE AND DAIRY FREE IDEAS

- My daughter, granddaughter, daughter-in-law, and sister eat dairy free and gluten free. I am just gluten free. Here are just a few suggestions that we like to use.

- My daughter always says to me: Mom, don't worry about me when you have desserts that have dairy or food items that have dairy at family dinners. Knowing this, I just try to have something that I know she likes and can eat on the menu too. It is hard to find good substitutes for creams, ice cream, butter, sour cream, etc. They can be found with hunting around and trying out new ideas and recipes. Earth Balance Butter is a butter substitute and there is coconut yogurt and ice creams.

- My daughter drinks the 30 calorie unsweetened Almond milk or So Delicious Coconut Milk. So Delicious Unsweetened Vanilla Coconut Yogurt is great to make a creamy breakfast shake.

- Breakfast Smoothie Recipe: 1/2 cup So Delicious unsweetened vanilla coconut yogurt, 1/3 cup applesauce, 3/4 cup pasteurized egg whites, 1 pkg. of sugar free or regular apple cider hot drink mix, vanilla, and 1-1/2 cup frozen sliced strawberries......Blend up and enjoy!

- My sister likes Earth Balance Butter Sticks.

- Rich's Whip is awesome for a cream or cool whip type product. It is in a carton like whipping cream and can be frozen or left in the refrigerator. You whip it up to use on things. Our Fresh Market Store's bakery uses it in the éclair pudding mix...My daughter gets it at the Kaysville Fresh Market at the bakery. She says that she has heard that stores might be starting to sell it.

- Her favorite treat: Cook and Serve Jello tapioca pudding made with almond milk and if she has some, Rich's whip on top. The cook and serve puddings are dairy free.

- Use Coconut oil to spread on toast....she likes it.

- Use coconut oil, regular oil, or olive oil in place of butter to sauté, cook eggs, etc.

- Marshmallows help to curb a craving for something sweet! My sister loves marshmallow crème in things, too.

- My daughter likes Jack's Links –Beef Steak (not beef jerky)—it is softer She gets them at Sam's Club and it has 12 g. of protein...so good when you need a snack and can't have cheese etc. anymore. She also eats dairy free protein bars-----She runs marathons and is also diabetic and so she needs protein to regulate blood sugars etc.

- Look for Sorbets to have instead of ice cream....make homemade or buy.

- Easy Cookies: Peanut Butter Cookies-----1 cup creamy or chunky PB, 1 cup brown sugar, 1 tsp. baking soda, 1 egg, 1 tsp. vanilla and 1/2 cup Dairy Free chocolate chips......mix up and drop on baking sheet. Bake 375 for 10 minutes. These are tender cookies. Let them cool about 5 minutes before removing. If you have some dark dairy free chocolate chips, you can add about 1/2 cup. Enjoy!

- We serve Rice-etti a lot....This is just spaghetti sauce over rice instead of noodles.

- Chicken Salad: 2 large cans of Costco chicken, 4 stalks celery, diced; 1/3 cup slivered almonds, 2 handfuls dried cranberries, Salt and Pepper to taste, 2 Tbs. Apple cider vinegar, 2-4 Tbs. or more mayo...Mix up and add mayo to good consistency. Eat this salad on Romaine lettuce leaf cups, on a bed of chopped Romaine, or on gluten free bread.

COOKING TIPS FROM JANEEN

AL DENTE:

* Italians say that al dente is "to the tooth". To test for doneness, remove a strand or piece of pasta and bite it--if it's barely tender to the bite but not to the core, it's done. It is slightly chewy and firm.

APPLES:

* There is about 1 cup of chopped apple in a medium apple

ANT/PEST SPRAY:

1 part white vinegar

1 part water

1. Pour equal amounts of water and white vinegar into a spray bottle and shake it to mix.
2. Spritz in areas where ants are common, such as kitchen floors, or crevices in baseboards. This can also be used outside.
3. Spray areas where guests are to come before they gather---picnic tables, porches, patios, etc.

ONE WHIFF ORGANIC BUG SPRAY:

Kills bugs and even squash bugs!

6 cloves garlic, finely chopped

1 small onion, finely chopped

1 Tbs. cayenne pepper

1 Tbs. liquid dish soap

1. Mix combination in 1 quart warm water, let it sit overnight.
2. Spray both sides of the plant leaves and all over the plant.

LAWN SPRAY:

1 can of beer (not light)

1 can of regular Coke (not diet)

1 cup ammonia

1. Mix in 20 gallon hose end sprayer.

2. Apply once a month.

AVOCADOS:

- Avocados do not ripen on the tree; they ripen or "soften" after they have been harvested.

- To speed up the avocado ripening process place unripe avocados in a brown paper bag with an apple or banana for two to three days until they are ripe.

- When avocados are perfectly ripe, wrap them in aluminum foil and place in the refrigerator. They will remain this way for several days and still be good.

BAKING POWDER

- 1 tsp. baking powder = 1/4 tsp baking soda plus 1/2 cup. buttermilk or sour milk to replace 1/2 cup of liquid in a recipe

BALSAMIC VINEGAR:

- 1 Tbs. balsamic vinegar is equal to 1 Tbs. cider or red wine vinegar plus 1/2 tsp. sugar

BASIL:

- A Basil bunch weighs about 2.5 ounces and has 60 sprigs. A sprig is 3/4 tsp. chopped.

- There is 1 cup of packed Basil leaves in a Basil bunch

- There is 1 cup of chopped Basil leaves in a Basil bunch

- There are 2 cups of loose Basil leaves in a Basil bunch

BEAN COUNTER:

A 1-lb. bag of dry beans will yield:

- 6-1/4 cups cooked black beans

- 7-1/2 cups cooked garbanzo beans (chickpeas)

- 6-1/4 cups cooked pink beans

- 5 cups cooked pinto beans

- 5 cups cooked red kidney beans

- 6-1/4 cups cooked white kidney beans

BROCCOLI HEADS EQUAL:

- There are about 2 Cups of Broccoli Stems Sliced in a Broccoli Head

- There are about 3-1/2 Cups of Broccoli Florets in a Broccoli Head

- A head of Broccoli looks like one trunk of a tree and a floret is like a branch of the tree.

- When buying Broccoli, it is usually packaged with 3 heads in an elastic band.

- A Broccoli crown is the head of the Broccoli with the bottom stems cut off.

BROWN SUGAR:

Two ways to make hard brown sugar soft again:

- Place the brown sugar in an airtight container with a slice of fresh bread placed on top. Seal and leave overnight. It should be soft and fresh again in the morning, if not just let it sit another day or two.

- Need soft sugar now? Quick Tip: Place the brown sugar chunk in a microwave safe plastic bag. Take a square of paper towel and moisten with water (not dripping wet–wring out excess). Place the wet paper towel in the bag with the sugar and seal. Place in the microwave for approximately 20 seconds. If still not soft, microwave for a few seconds more, repeating until the sugar is ready to use. Be careful not to melt the sugar.

Brown sugar can catch pests!

- With a butter knife, spread a dab of petroleum jelly on a small piece of cardboard, and then sprinkle it with brown sugar. Flies are drawn to brown sugar--then get stuck in the jelly. This can also be hung like the traditional fly paper--just punch a hole and insert twine.

Brown sugar acts as an anti-microbial and may prevent infection on small cuts from your razor, etc.

- Just clean the wound first with soap and water and then pack on the brown sugar.

Brown sugar is a great dead skin cell remover.

BROWN SUGAR DEAD SKIN CELL REMOVER

1/2 cup brown sugar

3 Tbs. olive oil

Pinch of nutmeg for fragrance.

1. Mix the above ingredients.

2. Wet your face or body, apply scrub in a circular motions for 1-2 minutes; wash off with warm water. Use this twice a week for smoother skin.

BUTTER:

- 2 Tbs. butter = 1 ounce

- 1 stick = 1/4 # or 1/2 cup

BUTTERMILK:

- 1 cup buttermilk is equal to 1 cup whole milk with 1 Tbs. lemon juice, stirred in well and let set for 5 min.

- 1 cup buttermilk is also equal to 2/3 cup yogurt or sour cream with 1/3 cup milk whisked in.

- Buttermilk will store 2 weeks in the refrigerator or 3 months in the freezer---Freeze your leftovers to use for the next time you need it.

CAKE FLOUR:

- 1 cup cake flour = 1 cups flour minus 2 Tbs. flour

CAN SIZES:

- 8 ounce can = 1 cup

- 12 ounce can = 1-1/2 cups

- No. 300 can or 14 to 16 ounces = 1-3/4 cups

- No. 303 can or 16 to 17 ounces = 2 cups

- No. 2 can or 20 ounces = 2-1/2 cups

- No. 2-1/2 can or 29 ounces = 3-1/2 cups

- No. 3 cylinder can or 46 fl. Oz. = 5-1/4 cups

- No. 10 can or 6.5 lbs. to 7 lb. 5 oz. = 12 to 13 cups or 5 No. 2 (20 oz) cans or 7 No. 303 cans

CAPERS:

- Substitute 1 Tbs. capers with 1 Tbs. chopped dill pickles or green olives.

CARROTS:

- 1 large carrot = 4 oz. = 1 cup grated

- 1 pound carrots = 1 average bunch = 6 to 8 medium or 4 very large = 3 cups chopped = 2&1/2 cups grated = 1 1/3 cups cooked and mashed

- 1 Pound Of Baby Carrots Is Equal To 2 Cups. 12 To 13 Baby Carrots Is 1 carrot

CATSUP:

- 1 cup catsup or chili sauce = 1 cup tomato sauce plus 1/2 cup sugar and 2 Tbs. vinegar (for cooked dishes only)

CELERY:

- One large (8 to 10-inch) stalk of celery will yield about 1/2 cup chopped celery.

CHEESE:

- 1 pound of cheddar cheese = 4 cups shredded
- 1/4 pound of blue cheese crumbles = 1 cup

CHICKEN:

Conversion of Raw Chicken in Pounds to Cooked Chicken in Cups

- 2 Chicken, skinless, boneless breast, cooked, cubed (2 medium) = 1-1/2 cups cooked
- 4-1/2 cups = a 3-pound chicken, cooked/diced
- Raw Chicken, 3/4 pound boned = 2 cups cooked and diced
- 2 cups cooked, cubed chicken = 1-1/2 pounds raw chicken breasts/bones
- To end up with four cups diced chicken, cook 1 ½ pounds of raw, skinless boneless chicken. Or, buy a cooked rotisserie chicken that weighs between 2-1/3 to 3 pounds. By the time you take off the skin and bones, you'll end up with the right amount or 4 cups.
- It may also be helpful to know that 4 cups of diced chicken will weigh about 20 ounces.

CHILI PASTE:

- 1 teaspoon chili paste is equal to 1/4 tsp. hot red pepper flakes

CHIVES:

- Chives are an herb, related to onions and garlic, with long green stems and a mild, not-too-pungent flavor. Chive plants develop bright purple blossoms which are edible and also have a mildly garlicky, oniony flavor. Chives are related to but not the same as garlic chives. Garlic chives have wider, flatter stems which are not hollow, and they have a rather pronounced garlic flavor.

- The green stems are the part of the chives that are used as an herb. Chive stems are hollow and are usually used fresh. Chives are typically chopped and can be used as a garnish, although they do have a mild oniony flavor, especially fresh ones.
  Chives can be featured in all sorts of recipes, from baked potatoes to soups, salads, sauces and omelets. They're frequently mixed with cream cheese to make a savory spread. Chive butter, a compound butter is made by blending chopped fresh chives into butter, and is frequently served with grilled steaks or roasted poultry.

- Chives are easy to dry for use in recipes in the microwave between two sheets of paper towels.

CHOCOLATE:

- 1 square (1 ounce) unsweetened chocolate = 3 Tbs. cocoa (dry) plus 1 Tbs. butter

CIDER VINEGAR:

- 1 tsp. cider vinegar is equal is 2 tsp. lemon juice with a pinch of sugar

CILANTRO:

- A Cilantro Bunch Equals about 93 sprigs and weighs about 2.8 ounces.
- There is 3/4 Cup of Cilantro Leaves Packed in a Cilantro Bunch
- There is 1 Cup of Cilantro Leaves Chopped in a Cilantro Bunch
- There are 1-1/2 Cups of Cilantro Leaves Loose in a Cilantro Bunch

CORNSTARCH:

- 1 Tbs. cornstarch = 2 Tbs. flour or 4 tsp. quick-cooking tapioca

CREAM:

- 1 cup whipping cream = 2 cups whipped

CROCK-POT TIMING CHART:

Good to know if you don't have access to a crock-pot or need to convert a recipe!

Conventional Cooking Time:	Crock-pot Cooking Time:
15 to 30 minutes	1.5 hours on High or 4-8 hours on Low
30 to 40 minutes	3 to 4 hours on High or 6 to 10 on Low
50 minutes to 3 hours	4 to 6 on High or 8 to 18 on Low

Most stews or roasts, pot roasts, and other uncooked meat/poultry and vegetable combinations will require at 8 hours on LOW or 4 to 6 hours on HIGH.

CRUMBS:

- 1-1/2 slice bread = 1 cup soft crumbs
- 1 slice bread = 1/4 cup fine dry crumbs
- 14 square graham crackers = 1 cup fine crumbs
- 22 vanilla wafers = 1 cup fine crumb

EGGS

- 1 whole egg = 2 egg yolks (for cooked custards)
- 8 egg whites = 1 cup
- 8 egg yolks = 3/4 cup

EGG SLICER IDEAS:

- These are not just great for eggs, but for mushrooms, strawberries, etc.

GARLIC:

- If you overbrown the garlic--just throw it out and start over----the dish will taste bitter.
- Bottled garlic can be used for fresh---not quite the same taste, but fast!
- 1/2 tsp. of bottled garlic is equal to 1 clove of garlic

GINGER:

- Buy fresh ginger in the produce department and then store in the freezer in a ziploc bag. No need to thaw when fresh ginger is needed for a dish. Just use your grater and grate away.

- To peel ginger when using a large piece, use the side of a spoon. (I don't peel ginger for a dish if using just a teaspoon or two.

HERBS:

- 1 teaspoon of dried herbs is equal to 1 Tbs. of fresh or 1/8 tsp. powdered herbs.

- Chop fresh herbs in a measuring cup with scissors if you have trouble with a chef knife. Using a chef knife is a great way, too.

- Strip leaves off rosemary, thyme, Oregano, Mints, Basil, and Tarragon before chopping. Don't use the stems unless you are floating the whole herb in the mixture.

- Wash herbs… If you know that you will be using herbs later in the day, spray off your fresh ones in the garden a few hours before and they will dry and ready to chop for your recipe without washing again.

- To help herbs last a few days longer, refrigerate them. Flat leaves or small stems can be gently wrapped in a damp paper towel and then sealed in a plastic bag.

- If you have larger quantities or for bigger herbs, like a bunch of basil, stand them upright in a glass in 1-inch of water before refrigerating. Cover loosely with a plastic bag. Can keep up to a week.

- To cut Basil, strip off the leaves, stack them, roll leaves up and slice thinly.

- Keep clipping off the herb's blossoms on your garden herbs because the herb's flavor changes some after blooming…

- Dry some herbs for winter use…cut a bunch with the stems and place an elastic band around the stems (about 1-inch thick) tightly and hang upside down in a dark place to dry. Strip leaves off and store in an air-tight container in the dark.

- If you have cut too many herbs for your dish, place extra chopped ones in an ice cube tray or combinations of them; add water and freeze. Pop these herb cubes into your recipes later.

- When using dry herbs, always crush them between your fingers to release the flavors as you add them to your dish.

- Add *Fresh* herbs about 10 minutes before your dish is finished cooking. In most cases, heat kills the flavor of fresh herbs, so they're best when added to a dish at the end.

- Dried herbs can be added at the beginning of cooking.

- Many supermarkets carry herb plants in their produce sections. Snip off as much as you need, and the plant will last for weeks or even months.

- To revive limp herbs, trim 1/2 inch off the stems, and place in ice water for a couple of hours.

- Wash herbs just before using; pat dry with a paper towel.

- More information and tips can be found in my book: Natural Growing, Cooking, and Preserving Secrets From the Herblady

HONEY:

- 1/2 cup honey is equal to 1/2 cup molasses or maple syrup

LEMONGRASS:

- 1 stalk of lemongrass is equal to 1 tsp. lemon zest

LEMONS/LIMES:

- 1 lime = about 2 Tbs. of juice and 1 tsp. of zest.

- 1 lemon = 2 Tbs. of juice and 1 Tbs. zest.

- To get more juice out of a lemon/lime, microwave it for 30 seconds before squeezing. Rolling lemons/limes on the counter before squeezing also helps to extract more juice.

- Zest the lemons before juicing. Freeze extra zest for future use.

- Squeeze half of a lemon in a glass of water and drink daily for its medicinal properties. It is a diuretic, helps flush toxins for those with arthritis and helps the liver be healthy plus lots more.

MEASUREMENTS:

3 tsp. = 1 Tbs.

4 Tbs. = 1/4 cup

5-1/3 Tbs. = 1/3 cup

8 Tbs. = 1/2 cup

12 Tbs. = 3/4 cup

16 Tbs. = 1 cup

1 cup = 8 ounces or 1/2 pint

2 cups = 1 pint

4 cups = 1 quart

4 quarts = 1 gallon

8 quarts = 1 peck

4 pecks = 1 bushel

1 ounce = 28.35 grams

1 grams = 0.035 ounces

1 quart = 946.4 milliliters

1 liter = 1.06 quarts

MEET TEMPERATURES:

BEEF & LAMB & VEAL:

Rare	140 degrees
Medium	160 degrees
Ground	160 degrees
Well-done	170 degrees (Lamb is 170 to 180 degrees)

CHICKEN/TURKEY:

165 degrees for breasts

175 degree for thighs

FRESH PORK:

170 degrees

SMOKED PORK:

Fully cooked:	140 degrees
Cook-before-eat:	160 degrees

MILK:

- 1 cup whole milk = 1 cup skim plus 2-1/2 tsp. butter
- 1 cup whole milk = 1/2 cup evaporated milk and 1/2 cup water

MUSHROOMS:

- Tip: store fresh mushrooms in a cool whip container with holes in lid in refrigerator.
- Don't ever soak mushrooms in water to clean them, just brush off and rinse.

MUSTARD:

- 1 tsp. dry mustard = 1 Tbs. prepared mustard

NUTS:

- 1 pound walnuts shelled = 1-1/2 to 1-3/4cups shelled
- 1 pound almonds in shell = 1-1/2 cups shelled

ONIONS/PEPPERS:

- Freeze extra chopped onion and bell peppers in ziploc bags for future use. I first freeze them on a baking sheet in a single layer. When frozen, transfer to the ziploc. This is great to do when peppers are a good buy at harvest time for winter cooking. This is also good for strawberries, blackberries, raspberries, blueberries, etc.
- Small onion = 4 ounces by weight or about 1/2 cup chopped or 1 Tbs. dehydrated
- Medium onion = 8 ounces, or about 1 cup chopped
- Large onion = 12 ounces, or about 1-1/2 cups chopped
- Jumbo onion = 16 ounces, or about 2 cups chopped

PASTA:

- There are 4 cups of dry pasta in one pound and 8 cups cooked.
- One cup dry yields 2 cups cooked.

PLAY DOUGH RECIPE:

3 cups flour

1 cup salt

2 Tbs. cornstarch

1-1/4 cups water

2 tsp. oil

Food coloring of choice

1. In a large bowl, combine flour, salt, and cornstarch. In a small mixing bowl, combine water and oil. Gradually stir water into dry ingredients until combined.

2. Knead until smooth. Divide dough into portions and knead in food coloring. (Add small amounts of water if the dough is dry or small amounts of flour if dough is too sticky.)

3. Keep dough in a ziploc bag to prevent drying out.

POTATOES:

- 1 pound of potatoes is 3 to 4 medium white potatoes, 7 to 9 small red potatoes, or 12 to 15 new or mini potatoes.

- One Potato Equals:

- There is 1/2 Cup of Potato Cooked/ Mashed in a Potato

- There is 2/3 Cup of Potato French Fries in a Potato

- There is 3/4 Cup of Potato Chopped in a Potato

- There is 1 Cup of Potato Sliced in a Potato

- There is 1 Cup of Potato Shredded in a Potato

RICE:

- One cup of uncooked long grain white rice is equal to 4 cups cooked rice. Medium grain rice yields only 3 cups.

- One pound of rice is 2 cups or 6 cups cooked. One cup of wild rice equals 2 cups cooked.

SAFFRON:

- 1/8 tsp. saffron is equal to 1/2 tsp. turmeric

RICOTTA RECIPE -- FRESH:

8 cups whole milk

Salt

Cheesecloth

3 Tbs. fresh lemon juice

1. Line large strainer with 4 layers of cheesecloth. Place lined strainer in a large bowl; set aside.

2. In a heavy-bottom 4 quart saucepan, heat milk and 1 tsp. salt to boiling on medium-high, stirring occasionally to prevent milk from scorching.

3. Stir in lemon juice; cover and remove from heat. Let stand 5 minutes. With slotted spoon, gently transfer curds from saucepan to lined strainer. Drain 3 minutes. Discard whey in bowl.

4. If not using right away, transfer ricotta to clean bowl, cover, and refrigerate up to 1 week. Makes 2 cups   Low-fat ricotta can be made with 2% milk instead of whole milk.

TAHINI:

- 1 cup tahini is equal to 3/4 cup peanut butter and 1/4 cup sesame oil

TOMATO JUICE:

- 1 cup tomato juice = ½ cup tomato sauce plus ½ cup water

TOMATOES:

- To cut cherry tomatoes in half, place them on a lid of a sour cream container. Top with another sour cream container lid. Place your hand on top of the lid, and using a serrated knife, cut them in half. Great for olives, grapes, etc. too!

- Tomato Equivalents:

  3 medium globe tomatoes = 1 pound

  8 small plum tomatoes = 1 pound

  25 to 30 cherry tomatoes = 1 pound

  2 cups chopped tomatoes = 1 pound

  3/8 cup of tomato paste plus 1/2 cup water = 1 cup tomato sauce

  1 cup canned tomatoes = 1-1/2 cups fresh, chopped, cooked tomatoes

  1/2 pound or 1 tomato = 1 serving

  1 cup firmly packed fresh tomato = 1/2 cup tomato sauce plus 1/2 cup water

  1 pound fresh = 1-1/2 cups chopped

  1 (16-ounce) can = 2 cups

  1 (35-ounce) can = 4 cups un-drained

  1 (28-ounce) can = 3 cups un-drained

- Too many tomatoes? Wash, stem, and place in a ziplock bag. Freeze.

  To use: Run frozen tomatoes under warm water to slip the skins. Allow to thaw or add to your cooked dish to thaw while cooking. This method can also be used with cherry tomatoes.

TORTILLA TIPS:

- Flour/corn tortillas: Heat one at a time in a dry skillet until lightly browned, 30 seconds per side.

- Soft corn tortillas: Wrap up to 6 in a damp towel and microwave on high until soft and pliable, about 20 seconds.

- Crispy corn shells for tacos: Microwave corn tortillas as directed, then brush each side with canola oil. To form the flat base and high sides for a taco, drape each shell over two parallel bars of the oven rack. Bake at 400 degrees until crisp, about 4 minutes. Transfer to a paper towel-lined plate (they will harden as they cool.

- To make flat tostada shells, brush both sides with canola oil and lay flat on oven racks until crisp.

- To make chips, brush tortillas with oil and then cut into 6-8 wedges. Lay them onto a cookie sheet and bake until crisp.

- Warming on the stovetop burner is another option. Put over the gas flame and turn often as blistered spots appear. When done, put into a dish towel and cover to keep warm.

WASABI:

- 1 tsp. wasabi is equal to 1 tsp. horseradish or hot dry mustard

WHITE SAUCE:

- Medium = 2 Tbs. butter, 2 Tbs. flour, 1/4 tsp. salt, and 1 cup milk = 1 cup sauce

- Thick = 3 Tbs. butter, 4 Tbs. flour, 1/4 tsp. salt, and 1 cup milk = 1 cup sauce

- Thin = 1 Tbs. butter, 1 Tbs. flour, 1/4 tsp. salt, and 1 cup milk = 1 cup sauce

- Melt butter over low heat, add flour and salt; add milk all at once. Stir until mixture thickens and bubbles.

YEAST:

- $1/3^{rd}$ of a 2 oz. cake compressed yeast = 1 package or 2 ¼ tsp. active dry yeast or enough to raise 3-4 c. flour.

ZIPLOC BAGS:

- Use these to marinate in, dredge meat or veggies, degrease sauces, a substitute pastry bag and also to store dry pantry foods as well as your leftovers.

JANEEN'S CLEANING TIPS

MAKING AND USING ANTI-BACTERIA, ANTI-VIRAL, ANTI-FUNGAL CLEANERS AND SPRAYS...

LAVENDER ANTIBACTERIAL SPRAY

1 cup water, distilled

20 drops pure essential oil of lavender

1. Pour the water into a spray bottle. Add the lavender essential oil and shake to blend.

2. Spray on the surface and let set for at least 15 minutes, or don't rinse at all. Makes: 1 cup spray. Shelf life: Indefinite

3. Great to take with on trips so that you can spray down your Hotels etc.

ALL-NATURAL ANTI-BACTERIAL SPRAY

1 cup water, distilled or filtered

5 drops orange essential oil

3 drops lavender essential oil

2 drops eucalyptus essential oil

2 drops tea tree oil

1. Mix and put into a spray bottle.

2. Spray surfaces and let air dry.

KITCHEN COUNTERTOP SPRAY

Use this fragrant solution to disinfect countertops, refrigerator shelves, and painted surfaces, including walls and wood trim. Feel free to experiment with other antibacterial essential oils, such as basil, thyme, or lemon.

1/2 cup distilled white vinegar

1/2 to 12 drops rose geranium or other scent essential oil

1. In a small, dark glass jar, combine the vinegar, water, and oil. Stir.

2. Pour small amounts into a spray bottle as necessary.

GENTLE SPEARMINT SCRUBBER

This is a non-scratching, chlorine-free paste is perfect for cleaning cookware, countertops, and porcelain sinks and tubs. Lemon and lemon verbena essential oils also work well in place of the spearmint.

1 cup baking soda

1 Tablespoon liquid castile soap

10 to 12 drops spearmint essential oil

Warm water (90° to 110°F)

1. In a small, dark glass jar, combine the baking soda, soap, and enough warm water to form a thick but pourable paste. Stir in the essential oil.

2. Apply to surfaces, wait for 5 minutes or more, then scrub with a sponge. Rinse off the residue with water.

ANTI-BACTERIAL BATHROOM CLEANER

Use this fragrant spray to disinfect bathroom surfaces. Tea tree (Melaleuca alternifolia) oil— which has antibacterial, antiviral, and antifungal powers—helps clean and control mildew. Lavender and hyssop, which were once used as disinfectant strewing herbs, have antibacterial and antiviral properties.

1/2 cup distilled white vinegar

1-1/2 cups water, distilled

2 Tablespoons liquid castile soap

8 to 10 drops tea tree essential oil

8 to 10 drops lavender essential oil

8 to 10 drops hyssop essential oil

1. Combine the vinegar, water, soap, tea tree oil, lavender oil, and hyssop oil in a dark glass jar. Stir.

2. Pour a small amount into a spray bottle to use as needed. Rinse off any residue with water.

HOMEMADE ANTI-BACTERIAL SOFT SCRUB CLEANSER

3/4 cup baking soda (you can add a little more if it seems a little thin after it's all mixed together.)

1/4 cup liquid castile soap (I used Dr. Bronner's Citrus Orange)

1 Tablespoon water, distilled

10-15 drops of Melaleuca essential oil (tea tree oil)

1 Tablespoon vinegar

1. In a medium sized bowl, combine the baking soda and castile soap. Add the water and tea tree oil and stir with a fork.

2. After the first 3 ingredients are well combined, SLOWLY add the vinegar. The mixture will bubble up because of the chemical reaction between the baking soda and vinegar.

3. Stir until you achieve a paste-like consistency. (I had to add a little more baking soda at this point until it was the "perfect" consistency.)

4. Transfer to a repurposed dish soap container (or any other container you prefer), grab your sponge and start cleaning!

WINDOW CLEANER

2 cups water, distilled

1/2 cup white vinegar

1/2 tsp. liquid dish soap

Blue coloring, if desired

1. Mix altogether in a spray bottle.

BLANK RECIPE PAGES

312

From the Kitchen of:

From the Kitchen of:

From the Kitchen of:

From the Kitchen of:

From the Kitchen of:

From the Kitchen of:

From the Kitchen of:

From the Kitchen of:

316

From the Kitchen of:

From the Kitchen of:

From the Kitchen of:

From the Kitchen of:

From the Kitchen of:

From the Kitchen of:

From the Kitchen of:

From the Kitchen of:

From the Kitchen of:

From the Kitchen of:

From the Kitchen of:

From the Kitchen of:

INDEX OF RECIPES

ABOUT THE AUTHOR

Janeen Pond (herblady13) is the author of 3 other cooking and gardening books:

1) TASTE TESTED AND APPROVED...*Delicious Main Dishes - Transforming Healthy Home Cooked Meals into Gluten Free Goodness the Whole Family will Love: Whether They Eat Gluten Free or Not !,*

2) TASTE TESTED AND APPROVED 2...*Scrumptious Soups, Salads, Snacks and Sides -Transforming Healthy Home Cooked Meals into Gluten Free Goodness the Whole Family will Love: Whether They Eat Gluten Free or Not !,* and

3) NATURAL GROWING, COOKING, AND PRESERVING SECRETS FROM HERBLADY13...*With Tips for Herbs, Vegetables, Healthy Cooking, Lawn Care, and Flowers, etc.*

 She is currently serving her second term as the President of the Tooele County Master Gardeners in the state of Utah. Janeen received her Master Gardener's Certificate in 2004 and has since received her Advanced Master Gardener's Certificate. Besides being a Master Gardener, her husband of 45 years, her 5 children, their spouses, and 17 grandchildren, have learned to garden, cook, and use her tips to help them to be more successful in their homes, kitchens, and yards. Janeen has also taught many classes on gardening, herbs, cooking, and flowers. Her family considers her to not only be a Master Gardener but also a master chef of home-cooked meals. While attending Brigham Young University and the University of Utah, her main focus of study was Foods and Home Economics.

She loves teaching other people how to grow, use, and cook with vegetables, fruits, and herbs. She is always finding something new to grow in her garden and a recipe to use it in. Janeen loves to be in her garden...but then comes right back into her kitchen to create a delicious meal from what she has gathered!

Made in the USA
San Bernardino, CA
18 July 2016